# CONNECTED

## *Finding My Truth*

# Diana Kayla Hochberg

CLASS

Publishing Division

# Connected: Finding My Truth
by Diana Kayla Hochberg

Copyright © 2025

ISBN 978-1-955095-48-8

Publishing Division
P.O. Box 2884
Pawleys Island, SC 29585
www.ClassAtPawleys.com

*This book is a work of non-fiction. Permissions have been obtained from those in the story. The information presented in this book is based on the author's best knowledge and understanding at the time of writing. The author has made reasonable efforts to ensure the accuracy and reliability of the information provided; however, errors and omissions may occur. Therefore, the author and publisher disclaim any warranty or representation, expressed or implied, concerning the accuracy, completeness, or usefulness of the information presented in this book. Some of the names of individuals and other identifying details have been changed to protect the individuals' identities. No generative artificial intelligence (AI) was used in this book to generate content. Furthermore, the author expressly prohibits any entity from using this publication for purposes of training artificial intelligence technologies to generate text.*

Library of Congress Certificate of Registration TX u 2-415-652

Printed in the U.S.A.

# DEDICATION

*To my son David, who brightens every day of my life
with his smile and laughter.*

*In memory of my father, Manny Hochberg,
who inspired me to chase my dreams: Let us soar.*

# CONTENTS

# FOREWORD

As a South Carolina physician, my days are filled with the stories of those who walk through my office door – each with a unique narrative, intricately woven from the diverse threads of their life experiences, health, and identity. My approach to medicine extends beyond diagnoses and treatments; I connect with individuals by understanding their stories to learn how to best to help them heal.

It was during one such encounter that I met Diana, and here is where her remarkable story begins. Diana offers us a front-row seat to her life full of unbelievable twists and turns, which she faced with resilience, courage, and the indomitable spirit of humanity.

*Connected – Finding My Truth* is not merely a recounting of events, it is a history, a mystery, and a profound family saga.

*Jason C. Rosenberg, MD*
*Board Certified by the American Board of Psychiatry and*
*Neurology in both Neurology and Pain Medicine*

# PROLOGUE
## *Las Vegas, Nevada, Spring 1993*

It had been three years since my husband's fatal accident, and I was still an emotional train wreck. Michele, my best friend since elementary school, kept urging me to meet her in Las Vegas for a few days, "for a break from things." My first thought was "No. I'm not ready." But I needed time with friends – friends who were like family.

So in the spring of 1993 my son David and I flew non-stop from Sarasota, FL to Las Vegas, NV.

And that's when it all started.

We met Michele, her husband Richard, and son Alex in the lobby of the Sahara Hotel. Michele and I were arm-in-arm, reminiscing about the good old days of teenage mischief and fun on the many trips Dad and I had made here with Michele along to keep me company.

Years later, here we were again, Michele and I, in Vegas. But my plans of dinner shows, spa days, and wine-laced lunches changed the evening I called Manny Diamond.

I knew Manny was a close friend of my father and a Vegas retiree. It had been awhile; I wanted to call to say I was in town, maybe suggest a cup of coffee. So I did. In retrospect, what transpired during that brief phone call should have set off an alert; after casual greetings and without prompting, Manny proceeded to recall some of my father's last days.

"I was at the hospital when your father died. Diana, I had begged him not to go to the Medical Center in the Bronx."

Dad died in the recovery room after an operation performed by a doctor who wasn't affiliated with the hospital.

"If Dad had listened to you, Manny, maybe he would be alive today."

Suddenly uncontrollable tears ran down my face. I tried to control my voice but the sorrow must have been audible because Manny changed the subject. He'd be at our hotel the following day.

At noon the next day Manny pulled up in a swanky Mercedes, and he drove us to Shari's on Buffalo Drive for lunch.

"You must be rich!" exclaimed David, tapping Manny on the shoulder.

Manny laughed. "I gamble a lot."

The smell of burgers and fries met us at the entrance. We slid into a booth with a table-top jukebox that entertained David as Manny and I swapped memories of New York and my parents' lake house.

I relaxed into a reminiscent trance.

"It's a shame you never got to meet your mother."

What? The trance broken, I thought I'd misunderstood, but I pretended to follow in hopes of clarification.

"Would you like me to help you find your biological parents?"

Excuse me? Mentally repeating the words to myself, I heard what he said. I stopped breathing for a moment and stared in disbelief.

"What are you talking about?"

My parents were Manny and Ethel Hochberg – indeed no strangers to me.

"Diana, I'm sorry. I didn't mean to say anything wrong. I assume you've never met your biological parents."

I felt sick to my stomach. I could hear my heart pounding. Immediately, he looked remorseful. But Manny Diamond's assumption was crushing me. Everything in my field of vision stopped. I felt hollow.

*Adopted?*

**I was adopted!?**

Little did I know how his gross misconception of what I knew about my family would change my life.

*Forever.*

# Chapter 1
## *Rescue Me from Vegas*

For the next five minutes, I heard nothing Manny said because this is what I knew: My parents were deceased. My mother was Ethel Hochberg. She passed from cancer before my eleventh birthday leaving her husband, my father, Manny Hochberg, to raise me alone. He did an outstanding job.

Yet questions lingered. *WAS this possible? Why should I listen to what this guy has to say? What if it's a bizarre truth and why hadn't Manny Diamond left it alone?*

And finally, I have to gather my courage and get out of here.

But Manny wasn't done.

"Diana, what happened to your husband? You are young. Are you okay?"

Who was this guy? What gave him the right to probe my past? I knew Manny as a friend of Dad's, but did I REALLY know him?

Before Steve's death, our marriage had struggled. We'd moved from Palm Springs back to our home in Sarasota, but Steve started a new job that kept him in California. Nine months later in a series of horrors, I filed for divorce, Steve died in a car crash in the desert, and I was left widowed with no monetary benefits.

No, Manny, I was NOT okay.

Manny switched topics, sharing war stories about his travels with Dad with a tantalizing delivery that enthralled David. Over ice cream and pie, the meal and evening ended with David begging for more stories about his grandfather, and Manny obliging on the drive back to the hotel.

My thoughts were scrambled. I was lost and confused. At the Sahara we expressed our gratitude and said goodbyes. My brain thudded dully. I called Michele to take David. I needed to be alone.

I took a long hot shower. Manny Diamond's words ran circles in my mind. After months of grief and trauma over an impending divorce and the consequences of Steve's death – just when I had FINALLY gathered the gumption to take my first steps toward healing, this man had shattered my fledgling sense of safety by suggesting a lifetime of memories with my family was a lie.

Wrapped in a plush hotel robe, I mixed a drink at the mini-bar and dialed my brother in New York. *Jesse Hochberg would settle this mess.*

When Jesse finally picked up, I filled him in on the evening and my conversation with Manny Diamond. And my questions began to fly.

"Where were you when I was born?"

"That's a long time ago, Sis, but I believe I was visiting Aunt Rebecca … yeah, her girls – our cousins … Susan and Eve were there, too."

"Was Mommy pregnant?"

"Gee, Diana … I was a kid… I never thought about stuff like that. Have you looked at your birth certificate?"

"Well, no. I don't have a birth certificate."

"That's odd. How did you get your driver's license? You have a Social Security card, right?"

I thought about it. Daddy had always taken care of everything – I had a driver's license, and was never asked for more.

When Steve and I got married and even when I did court work with judges – my driver's license was enough. It was odd, now that it came to mind.

Jesse's voice interrupted my musing …

"Diana, Manny Diamond must be wrong. I don't know what makes me feel that way other than I know for a fact Dad and Manny Diamond had words at the end."

What? This, too, was news. What words had transpired between Manny H and Manny D? Jesse suggested I order a copy of my birth certificate from New York State and we hung up.

Jesse gave me a glimmer of hope … a hope that Manny Diamond had lied.

# Chapter 2
## *Rescue Vegas from Us*

The stress of the last day had taken a toll. I needed a break. While Michele's mom looked after the boys, the adults dressed for a night out. We enjoyed a fantastic dinner complete with tableside magician. In the midst of all the crazy information I'd been slammed with, I could use some magic.

As the evening wound down we settled at the bar for a nightcap – or two – and Michele and I continued our walk down Memory Lane. Richard was all ears and I had the floor.

"My first trip to Vegas with Dad was in November '67 for the annual auto show. Mom passed away in March the year before, Jesse was away in the Army, and I was too young to be left alone for a week, so Daddy took me. He was fascinated with the constant changes in Vegas. As the city grew, each new hotel seemed more glamorous, the rooms more extravagant. Every year, we stayed in a different hotel. Caesar's Palace. The Dunes. And he insisted on a top floor with a city view. He knew Vegas was no place for a child or a teenager, but we had no other options. So Michele came along for company."

She added, "We started our day at the pool. In the afternoons, we'd catch a movie or hit the mall. And we hung around the casinos to people-watch."

I piped in, "Yeah, yeah! I remember once we spotted a man blowing on his dice for good luck and another crossing his fingers with both hands in the air. I looked at you and said,

'Michele, we can do this!' So, we walked over to a slot machine and put in three quarters. Immediately, a man leaned over and tapped you on the shoulder. We turned around, and it was a security guard."

Richard found his voice. "You girls, I swear. Didn't you know better?"

"Nope. He said he assumed we didn't see the signs about being twenty-one or older to gamble. Remember how we thought he was trying to act tough? I kept waiting for him to crack up but he was serious and told us what we did was illegal and the fine was a thousand dollars each PLUS jail!"

Michele took the lead. "By then, tears were pouring down our faces. We apologized over and over and begged for forgiveness. Finally, he barked, 'OK, get out of here, I don't want to see either of you back.' He looked at Diana and said, 'I know your father; he is a good client of this hotel.' We looked at each other and took off to the room, feeling lucky."

"I guess that cured you two."

I laughed. "Oh no. It gets better. The next day we went to the hotel beauty salon and told the receptionist we needed new hairdos and manicures for the night. She eyeballed us up and down and said she was booked …"

"… that's when Michele whispered loudly, 'Oh, Diana! I guess she doesn't know who your father is. When he finds out, will he be upset! We could have gotten her backstage.'"

"Following her lead, I said, 'Oh, yes.' As we walked out, the lady stopped us. Excuse me ladies, I just had two cancellations."

"Michele and I were giggling. We were seated and given the royal treatment, with the bill charged to the room. As soon as we thought we were safe inside our room, the phone was ringing. It was the salon. Daddy answered …"

"Hello, Mr. Hochberg?"

"This is Manny Hochberg."

"This is Wanda, from the hotel beauty salon downstairs, calling to confirm your information."

"What are you talking about?"

"We took excellent care of your young ladies downstairs in the salon today," Wanda said. "They were polite and mentioned you were performing at the hotel tonight."

"What excellent care do you mean?"

"Shampoo, style, blow-dry, and manicures. When should I come up to get my passes for tonight's performance?"

"Did they tip you?"

"No tip was necessary – because of the passes."

"I'll be down in an hour." Dad was clearly outraged. He went to the show lounge and bought two tickets. And when he came back he was even madder. We tried to disappear into the couch.

"*You girls are grounded.* No pool. No movies. No nothin'."

At this point he'd had enough of us. He called Michele's mom and told her she needed to come to Vegas pronto. Nancy arrived and order was restored but the deed was done. No one could take away that memory.

Dad had Vegas adventures, too. He told stories about playing craps at 3 AM with Elvis. He took us to a late-night Ann Margaret show with dinner afterwards – after midnight! He proclaimed, "There are no clocks in Vegas! You eat whenever and whatever you want! It's Vegas!"

It was an interesting trip to say the least. The best part was reuniting with Michele; the worst part was Manny Diamond's bizarre "revelation."

I knew once I was home in Florida I'd be able to figure everything out and move on. There had to be an explanation.

# Chapter 3
## *Confidential*


Back home in Sarasota, Florida, I called the NY State Department of Health about my birth certificate. Two months passed with no response. So I called again. I was told it should be mailed by the end of the week.

Meanwhile, I met Dean, a single father of a boy in David's Tae Kwon Do class. The four of us began hanging out. I told him about Las Vegas. He suggested I ask relatives and friends of my parents. So I made a list and started calling.

I contacted Mom's cousin Esther and pretended I was aware of my adoption.

"Diana, leave it alone. You're opening a can of worms."

"Come on, Esther, is it true?"

All I heard was, "Good night." We never spoke again.

Next, I called Jon Russo, dad's friend and foreman at the factory. He seemed glad to hear from me, expressed condolences about Steve, and asked if there was anything he could do.

"As a matter of fact there is. Did you know about my adoption?" There was a long pause.

"I need to speak to my lawyer. I'll be in touch."

"Really? It's a few simple questions. Why do you need a lawyer?"

There was a change in his voice. "I drove your father that day."

"Drove my father where on what day?"

"I'll give you a call later."

He never called back.

This was becoming the norm – my questions met with silence. And it did nothing but make me more determined.

Next was Dad's lawyer, Nathan Costello. Seeing his name reminded me of a conversation my brother had with Dad before he went to the hospital. According to Jesse, our father had retained another lawyer to put together a new will. My brother's take on the exchange did not paint Nathan in the best of light.

"Nathan was stealing money from the business. He had cost Daddy thousands and thousands of dollars. He stole from our inheritance, and his advice was not in Dad's best interest. By the time the new will was officiated, Dad had passed, and Nathan became the Executor of Daddy's will. We got screwed."

With this in mind, I dialed the Nathan's number. A woman answered.

"Hello, this is Diana Hochberg. Do you remember me?"

"Yes I do. You're Manny's Diana. Please, call me Rosalind." After small talk I got down to business. Nathan had died in 1985, so I asked Rosalind point blank:

"I know it might be a long shot, but do you know about my adoption?"

Her voice softened and she paused. "I need to speak to our son first. I'll see if he can look through his father's records and find the files on the three of you."

"What do you mean 'the *three* of us'?"

"I'll call you back. Give me a week or so."

I continued the calls, changing my spiel in each conversation, hoping to get different answers. But all the answers – if I could get any answers at all – were the same. It seems no one in the family knew, or would admit to knowing, that we had been adopted.

Back to square one. Maybe Manny Diamond was full of it.

I searched through Dad's belongings again, looking through all the papers and photos for a clue I'd might have overlooked. No luck.

Then it hit me: The attic in Dad's factory. Those suitcases. I assumed Jesse had checked them out years ago after Daddy passed; it turned out we'd both forgotten.

So I called the guy who'd bought the factory from Daddy '78. It turned out he had found a small binder with Dad's initials when he cleaned out the attic.

"I never heard from you or Jesse after the funeral, and I didn't know how to get in touch so I kept it, hoping to hear from you. What's your address?"

A few days later the package with a weathered binder came. Inside were a few photos from Dad's Army days, some postcards, and an eleven-page handwritten letter from Joe Klein to Daddy.

One of the sentences read, "You should have told Ethel the truth. Hoc, you should have trusted me and taken my advice." The next day I made a copy and mailed the original to Joe Klein in Beverly Hills.

*Did my father have a scandalous affair? Did he know my mother?*

A week later, Joe Klein called.

"Hi, Joe. I'm guessing you received the letter."

"Yeah I received it. And when I did, I knew something was up. I was afraid to tell you things before … I didn't want to hurt you."

"Afraid to tell me what, Joe? That Manny adopted me?"

Joe let out a sigh. "Your father never adopted you. It was complicated. Your biological mother wasn't willing to relinquish all her rights, and Manny never told Ethel the truth; she never knew it wasn't legal."

"It's okay. I want the truth." Then for whatever reason I told him I had always thought of him as a decent guy. He thanked me for that, wished me good luck, and told me to call if I had any questions.

Well, I had questions aplenty. That was for sure.

The next day a letter came from New York's Department of Health stating my birth certificate had been amended several times. A man named Randy was assigned to my case. According to him the document named my father as Manuel Hochberg, thirty-eight years old, and my mother, Ethel Eres, twenty-four. My place of birth was listed as Manhattan General Hospital, Manhattan, Kings County, New York. He sent this first certificate, listing Mom and Dad's names as I had been told. The spaces for my date of birth as well as my first and middle names were blank. There was another line labeled "Number of children born alive:" it read, "None."

Well, this was wrong. I knew for a fact Dad was forty-five, and Mom/Ethel was forty.

Baffled by the document's errors, I decided to reach out to Manny Diamond, letting him know how hard his claim that I might be adopted had rocked my world, shattering every reality I'd ever known. And how my subsequent research was leading me on a wild goose chase and yes, as much as I hated to ask for it, I needed his help.

He told me again he hadn't meant to hurt me ... that while he was in the Navy he'd worked as a CIA agent. I guess he thought that would make him seem qualified to investigate. At this point, I was ready to get on with it. I was itching for the truth.

The annual auto show in Vegas is a big deal; Manny wanted me to go. He was sure my father's business colleagues and friends would be in attendance, a ripe gathering of possible informants for my quest. Of course he was going, so I agreed. He said he would call me later to see if I had learned anything.

After that, Manny contacted me every few days.

Meanwhile, it had been over a week, so I called Rosalind. She was pleasant and forthcoming.

"Do you remember last week when I told you there were three children?"

How could I forget?

"Manny and your Uncle Abraham each adopted a baby, but one never was. Of the two who were, one was adopted through New York City Jewish Services and the other through Catholic Services. The mother of the third refused to sign any papers."

I didn't get it. "What are you telling me?"

"Diana, the boy was legal, Jewish, and adopted by Manny and Ethel. One girl was given to Manny's brother, Abe. I don't know which of the two girls was Jewish; that's all I could find out."

I thanked her and asked her to stay in touch. I hoped she'd find more.

For the next few weeks I was edgy with anticipation of the next bombshell. Manny Diamond finally called. He had scheduled dinner with Mort Shulman.

The same day I received another birth certificate and called my caseworker, Randy. This document had "D.K." by my name.

Randy was indeed swamped; he had fifty-one cases to close by month's end and my circumstances were not unique among them. He had turned up no evidence of my adoption in New York and the subject of my birth certificate was closed.

"But Randy, I have a right to know the truth."

"Let it be," he replied.

I called my cousin, Roberta Hochberg, the other legally adopted child, but I needed to be gentle – I didn't want her blindsided as I had been. Roberta's marriage had recently collapsed – finding out that she was adopted might send her over the edge.

At first we talked about our years growing up together … Sundays at her house and conversations with her mom. Roberta's folks were older than mine, and I was older than Roberta. Before Roberta, Aunt Anna had suffered five miscarriages so she always called Roberta her "miracle baby." I thought how hard that must have been on Aunt Anna. She was a sweet lady and loved me like her own.

After we caught up, I explained what had happened in Vegas, the trouble I'd had researching my birth certificate, and how Jesse fit in the scenario. I tried to be compassionate. Though my delivery was much gentler than Manny Diamond's outburst had been, she couldn't help but be shocked and found it as unreal as I had.

"You've got to be kidding, Diana. I remember Nathan. Have you been able to reach him?"

I told her Nathan had passed, and that his wife, Rosalind had been the first person to mention three children and the notion of adoption.

"She's wrong. Think about it, Diana. Look at our features. It's obvious we're related. Look at Grandma Molly's photo; you look just like her at that age. Give me Rosalind Costello's number. I'll straighten this out."

Roberta didn't wait for me – she found Rosalind's number on her own and Rosalind gave her the same information I had received.

When the mail arrived on November 19, 1993, there was a piece from the New York Department of Health with CONFIDENTIAL stamped in large red letters and postmarked November 17, 1993.

It was my most recent birth certificate. This time the name was listed as Karen Diane.

# Chapter 4
## *"Girls Just Want to Have Fun"*

"Girls Just Want to Have Fun" started playing in my head as I opened my eyes on a Friday morning reminding of easygoing times with girlfriends times before I met Stephen.

I was four months into my pregnancy when I met Stephen, who would later become my husband. After my baby boy arrived, Stephen's daughter from his previous marriage, Claire Marie, made us a unit of four.

Tragedy struck seven years later when Stephen died in a car accident in the California desert. Overwhelmed by grief, I mourned deeply. When Claire Marie's mother moved back to Germany, she claimed custody and whisked Claire away with her.

It felt like another death.

As hard as it was, I somehow managed as a single parent as David and I navigated our new normal. I tried to stay cheerful for him – and for me. I couldn't wallow in despair … I steeled myself to seek joy and embrace good times.

It was a spur-of-the-moment decision to call my happy-go-lucky girlfriend Stacey. We were friends from back in the day and her high spirits had always been contagious.

"Let's go out tonight and have some fun," I proposed.

Stacey didn't skip a beat when she agreed. "I'm in, Diana, let's do it!"

We went a bit wild on November 19, 1993. As I dressed for the evening, I glanced at my wedding ring, took it off, and stashed it safely in a dresser drawer.

The night got started with a late dinner and drinks. Laughter and joking filled the air. I flirted with a cute bartender and we spent a good part of the night on the dance floor letting off steam. We must have danced our cares away; once we were back in our seats, we relaxed and started talking about our lives. It was nice to have a girls' conversation. We both worked full time. I was a devoted single parent. Her husband was a Merchant Seaman on a submarine for six months at a time.

I told her about the research I was doing, how time consuming it was, and how I had been led to doubt that Manny and Ethel were my biological parents. I told her I was trying to move past the shock and approach this new information with a sense of adventure. We chatted more about old times over another drink and decided we weren't quite ready to head home.

At a late-night party on Siesta Key, there was more dancing – and much more flirting. I ran into a guy I knew years before I was married. He asked for a dance. We were having a good time and laughed when "Girls Just Want to Have Fun" came on. Stacey and I gave each other a look; it was high time to head home. We laughed and danced our way off the floor and ducked out the back.

When we pulled up to my house the front door was open. I stopped dead in my tracks, then turned on my heel and sprinted back to the car, terrified. Stacey was already calling the cops. All the commotion roused the neighborhood. The police arrived and went in first. When I was finally allowed inside what I saw was a scene from a crime drama … paintings askew, photos torn from walls, furniture overturned, cushions and books scattered across the floor … drawers and cabinets dumped, their contents strewn all around. My bed's pillowcases had been stripped off – I imagined them full of my jewelry and valuables, slung over the masked looters' shoulder as they scurried into the night. Someone was looking for something, and in a hurry to find it.

When the losses were tallied they included a cherished collection of music boxes, various items from my desk drawers and file cabinet, all my jewelry, and my wedding ring. The pit in my stomach grew as I realized its absence: it was weird that it was stolen the very first day I'd removed it since Stephen's death.

When asked, I valued my missing jewelry at $60,000. The looks from the officers made me feel like a suspect, like I was pulling an insurance con.

I was incensed, loudly demanding badge numbers, the names of their supervisors. The nerve of the implied accusation was like a slap in the face.

My home was in shambles from a violent invasion. I was physically shaken. I had been violated. Strangers had been in my bedroom, plundering my privacy. What was once my place of safety was now a public crime scene.

I was trying to calm down when I realized my adoption-related paperwork –photographs, news clippings, phone lists, recordings, notes, the birth certificates – all of it – was gone. The only things left were my journals – and only because I'd left them in the trunk of my car by accident.

My mind picked through the last few days and the phone calls. I'd thought little of them until now. Pranks. Telemarketers. There seemed to be no pattern to the hang-ups … but the messages with intense breathing on my answering machine gave me pause and they continued after the burglary.

David came home Sunday, his eyes widening at the chaos from the break-in.

He went out back to play only to turn back to report a

large gap in our fence. "Mom, there's a big hole in our fence and a part of it is knocked down. What happened here? Why is the house such a mess? Where are my Nintendo games?"

When I told him about the robbery, I tried not to make a big deal out of it. But I heard his screams in the middle of the night and when I raced to comfort him he couldn't stop saying someone was in his room; the intruders has returned to take him. I let him sleep with me for three weeks. He kept close to home. He was terrified.

My neighbor installed floodlights and sat on his front porch every night with a rifle for a month. Finally his wife convinced him to invest in a state-of-the-art alarm system. Our once-tranquil community was now regularly patrolled by cops and full of signs ...

*Warning Neighborhood Watch.*

# Chapter 5
## *Answering Machine*

Every time the phone rang, my heart would race, hoping it was either Manny Diamond or Mort Shulman. I couldn't sleep. I'd wake in the middle of the night and clean house to pass time, the coffee set to brew at 6:30 AM.

So I don't know how I missed the call, but I finally heard his voice on the answering machine … "Diana, it's Manny. I learned about your parents. Mort Shulman will call with details."

Mort later left a brief message: "Hello, Diana. This is Mort Shulman. I have information about your mother. I'll call Thursday at 9 PM."

The phone rang promptly at 9 PM Thursday. He made small talk before he started in on what I wanted to know. He apologized for not attending the funeral, citing some lame reason about his mistress being afraid he would start a conversation that would be inappropriate. I wasn't listening. I was ready for some truth.

"You've known me all my life, yet you haven't seen fit to tell me I was adopted? I don't get it. Why?"

"You're right. And I can't change that. But I'm telling you now. Your mother's name was Donna Kolosky. She was a hat-check girl in a Montreal jazz club I use to hangout in. One night I asked her out for coffee after her shift. I could tell something was bothering her. We had talked enough at the

21

club for me to know she had moved to Montreal from Vancouver. When I asked Donna about her move, she clammed up and we parted ways for the night."

"Two months later, she asked me out for coffee and confided in me. She was four months pregnant and she wanted to keep it. 'Mort, the baby needs to be safe.' She wanted her child to grow up in a nurturing environment. Donna was remarkable, so much more than a pretty face; she was intelligent and driven."

"Was she Jewish?"

"I thought so. When I met your mother, she introduced herself as Donna Cole. I told your parents she was Jewish.

"I knew Manny and Ethel wanted to adopt. After the war Jewish couples in the States had limited legal options. I knew about a NY agency that specialized in Jewish adoptions; Manny and Ethel expressed interest. Like many other couples across the country, the waiting lists were long. I suggested black-market adoptions. It was risky, but the results were promising. I mentioned Donna, explained she was Canadian from Vancouver, and her family lineage was Ukrainian, Austrian, and Polish. We thought she was the perfect candidate. The child was due in September, and we planned to bring Donna down to New York City, which was tricky: she was nine months pregnant; getting her across the border would take some doing."

And he stopped there in the middle of his tantalizing tale about my life to say he needed to speak to his lawyer before he said more – because he was a convicted felon. Wow. I wished he had thought about this before leading me on, but I was in no position to complain. He clearly held vital pieces to my puzzle. I wanted to hear more.

I poured a glass of wine and pulled out Dad's memorabilia … a Canadian Flag pin, a 1967 Royal Canadian Mounted

Police maple leaf spoon, and Canadian coins. I wondered if these had belonged to Donna.

A few days later, Mort left a message on the answering machine. I called back on his private line.

"My attorney says I can't be prosecuted for helping Donna cross the border. The statute of limitations has passed."

"Where did you take her when you crossed?"

"Plattsburgh, NY. We passed through border patrol pretending to be a family. We met your father and his foreman in Lake Placid for the exchange. Ethel wasn't there."

"What happened next?"

"Although Donna made a deal to give you to the Hochbergs, she really wanted you. I had to agree to have photos sent through me every year. There's no birth certificate anywhere naming Donna as your mother. There's a fake document that lists Manhattan General as your place of birth instead of Montreal. It lists Manny and Ethel as your birth parents. Your parents' ages are incorrect. Your mother refused to sign any papers. I assured her she didn't need to; the arrangement was money for her college tuition, dental work, and a one-way flight back to Vancouver in exchange for you becoming a Hochberg."

"So I was I born in Montreal?"

"That's right, and you were conceived in Vancouver."

"Did you have an affair with my mother?"

I thought I heard a muffled snort. "Your mother was an intelligent woman, she knew I was nothing but a ladies' man. She refused to give me a chance."

"Why did my mother give me up?"

"It wasn't an easy decision. It was the '50s, so she was facing many challenges. She didn't reveal your father's identity but did tell me he was Italian.

"During a business trip to Toronto I found her in the lobby of my hotel. There she was by the elevators when I came out. She'd been waiting for hours. She made a catty remark about 'keeping a lady waiting,' then started to vent that my part in your adoption was a felony. That everything was my fault. I reminded her that she had accepted the money and agreed to the terms.

"I think what she was after was a place to live while she attended university in Montreal. I knew a friend with a spare room in the city, and she agreed to take it. All the while she wanted to get her baby back. After she got a degree in accounting, I gave her a job. Then her sister Jan showed up, freshly divorced and full-on mad at the world, making her hard to like and even harder to deal with. But she ended up rooming with your mother and working for me, too. It was hard to say no to Donna. She knew I was a womanizer and unfaithful to my wife and my mistress Andrée, too. But she had secrets and plans of her own …," his voiced drifted. I could tell he was finished talking. We hung up.

After the call, I searched Vancouver for traces of Janet Koloski, but all I found was a listing for Tom Kolosky. I dialed the number, introduced myself, and asked if he knew Jan Kolosky. Turns out Jan was his sister. She'd remarried and had taken her husband's name.

Tom was nice, easy to talk to, and kind enough to give me Jan's contact info. I thanked him and we hung up. Then I realized I had unintentionally recorded the entire exchange and decided to listen again. That's when it sunk in: I had talked to my biological uncle for the first time.

I prepared myself before I called Jan. After Mort's description of her, I wanted to tread lightly. A woman with a raspy voice answered, and when I spoke, I threw my prepared caution to the wind and cut right to the chase. I needed information.

"Hello, my name is Diana. I'm Donna's daughter; I'm your niece."

"Who is this? Where do you live?"

"I live in Florida."

The voice became downright hostile. "My niece lives in New York City, not Florida."

"I'm from New York; after I graduated college, I moved to Florida to teach for a year, and I stayed."

"You are not my niece. I don't recognize your name!" The phone slammed down and the call was over.

The conversation didn't go as planned but it was clear she was aware of my existence and where I grew up. I started sensing Mort was right about her. She was horrible. Her voice had gone from cold to nasty. Several days later, she called back.

She apologized, said that I had surprised her. That though she had known this day would come, my call caught her unprepared. I told her I hadn't meant to shock her. She asked for my address and began sending letters, describing Donna and the rest of the family ...

*December 1, 1993*

*Dear Diana,*

*Your call was a wonderful surprise. I thought one day I'd hear from you after Mort Shulman told me all about you. He arranged everything for Donna and your adoption. On October 8, 1937, Donna was born at Royal Columbian Hospital in New Westminster, the youngest in our family. There were two boys, Freddie, and Ronnie, and two girls, Dorothy and me. Our father is dead, but Mom is still with us at eighty-three. Donna's given name was Camilla Marilyn Koloski. Because none of us liked the name Camilla, we renamed her Donna.*

*She left home at an early age and went to live in Montreal. After she graduated from McGill University, Mort gave her a job to help her get established.*

*Your mom was a lovely person in every way. She had a sense of humor enhanced by a beautiful smile. She loved dogs. Coco, a Havanese, was her favorite. She once had a white poodle named Caesar. Donna was active in sports and fluent in several languages. She was an avid skier and swimmer.*

*I still miss Donna. Her death was a shock and unexpected; she was young. She passed away on May 10, 1967, at Vancouver General Hospital. The autopsy showed inflammation of the heart with rheumatic scarring.*

*I'm glad to share more. We would love to hear more from you. Here are some pictures of Donna; I'll try to find more. We've all lost many years and are grateful you found us.*

*Your Aunt Jan*

I was thrilled. This was a lot of information; I was pleased she was willing to share. I know I read that letter more than ten times that night. I had mixed feelings. She didn't tell me everything, and I didn't blame her. We both had our guards up, and I was vulnerable. I took it slow, keeping it light when I wrote or called. Each letter shed new light and brought me closer to my mother. I researched Vancouver and my new family. After several letters, I felt we had moved in the right direction. Jan and I enjoyed our conversations with each other. I had accepted my new family. The timing felt right, I was ready for Vancouver.

During the next nine months, I made life-changing decisions. I learned about my Canadian family and where they lived, and I studied everything about the area. I completed travel school and took a job with Continental Airlines in Tampa, Florida.

I befriended a co-worker, Kathy White-Fuller. She lived in Clearwater and encouraged me to move there when David finished elementary school, citing great schools with high scholastic test scores. It wasn't hard to convince me to make a fresh start – it was great timing for David and me. And

Continental Airlines provided excellent benefits and perks … I could travel the world! I rented out our Sarasota house, and we moved to Clearwater. Changing schools disrupted David's routine but he bounced back, made new friends and came to love it.

And I planned our first trip to Vancouver.

# Chapter 6
## *First Trip to Vancouver 1994*

I wasn't sure what to expect when I planned the trip to Vancouver to meet my blood relatives in the summer of '94; I vowed that, if things became uncomfortable, David and I would leave.

I booked a flight to Seattle and a rental to take us to the ferry. It was David's first time out of the country and he was excited; the ferry captain was friendly and entertaining, encouraging us to look for whales or dolphin. David was into it; and it was a pleasant enough distraction but I was on quest – a fact-finding mission for clues to unravel the mystery Manny Diamond's words had stirred up.

Aunt Jan was waiting in the yard when we drove up.

"Donna!"

I gave her a long hug. "I'm Diana."

"It's incredible how much you look like her. This must be David."

The grounds offered a panoramic view of the mountains. The enormous dining room table was set for ten. The master bedroom was on the main level with three more bedrooms upstairs. One specifically made my heart sing; the furniture was Art Deco. I love Art Deco. As it turned out, the furniture in this room was Mom's.

The more my aunt talked, the happier I was to know my mother and I shared interests; for the first time, my aunt was realizing I was Donna's daughter.

Her husband Orland was friendly. "Hi, I'm Orland, Jan's better half. And you must be David. Son, do you like horses?"

"I like horses, cats, sharks, and lions."

"There are no sharks or lions here, but I have race horses and barn cats."

Orland told us how he started as a horse groomer in 1965 and in 1978, became a trainer. As if on cue, we were hustled about for a trip to the local racetrack – Hastings – where we spent the rest of the evening. I was intrigued by this pastime. Is this MY family? Are they all into horse racing and gambling?

Back at the house we were shown our sleeping quarters – and they weren't upstairs. I ducked my head to miss a crossbeam as we headed down creaking stairs into a dusty basement with two double beds where Aunt Jan wished us good night.

"Breakfast is at 7 AM. See you in the morning."

We got ready for bed. I found it strange that David and I were sleeping in the basement of a four-bedroom house of our newly found family. I mean, this wasn't exactly an ideal welcome. Then I thought about Jan … how traumatic losing a sibling must have been – and how disturbed she was that I looked so much like her. And I remembered Mort's comments of how jealous Jan was of Donna.

At breakfast the table was meticulously set and laid out with family photo albums, and Aunt Jan talked about mom and family. My aunt was vague about details.

"When will we get to meet my grandmother and Uncle Tom?"

"In a few days, I'll call Tom. Mother had five children, Donna was the youngest. Ron left home at fourteen for Vancouver Island to be a lumberjack. He stayed until the mid-70s. Freddie lives with Mother and takes care of the house. He was in the service for many years and is fluent in several languages:

Freddie and your mom could both read and write in six languages. My sister Dot lives in Langley with her roommate, Marty Holmes. Dot divorced her husband, Mike, in the '70s. She's quite fond of country living and has a beautiful flower garden."

"That's amazing; which languages did she speak?"

"English, French, Ukrainian, German and Italian, with a basic understanding of Spanish. Freddie was fluent in Japanese, Spanish, Mandarin, Russian, and English."

I had more questions, but my aunt had already made plans for us; there was no time to linger. She drove around narrating town history. After a stop at Science World, we headed back to the racetrack. Horses and racetracks, racetracks and horses ... despite my growing curiosity about our family, their racetrack obsession was making it hard to uncover information.

My aunt said we'd talk more about family in the morning. Was she becoming more comfortable with me? Reading her wasn't easy.

In the morning I sent David outside to the garden while Jan and I talked.

"Your mother enjoyed luxury – high-end fashions and exquisite jewelry. She wore a gold Swiss watch daily. She was passionate about swimming, skiing, and travel. Donna liked to try everything – horseback riding, skating, tennis ... she enjoyed antiquing and reading bestsellers. She made us all proud as a college graduate. Languages came naturally to her; she never married or smoked. She attended St. Paul's Anglican Church. And your mother hated growing up poor.

"Dad passed from lung cancer when he was 67. Mother is 84. The only thing wrong with her is cataracts. I don't have a name for your father, but he was from Vancouver – a gambler of Italian descent, as far as we know."

I sat with Jan while she spoke of my mother and I sensed she was only sharing parts of the story.

"What happened to my mom? How did she die?"

"Why? It was unexpected and sudden." Jan's voice was tinged with sorrow.

"Where is she buried?"

"Forest Lawn, in Burnaby, about ten minutes from here,"

"When was the last time you visited?"

"Never."

Did I hear right? Never? There was silence.

"How about the rest of the family?"

"On Christmas Day, 1972, your Uncle Ron went out on a blind date with a gal named Jeanne. Two years later, they married on Christmas day. It was romantic."

I tried to steer the conversation towards something less contentious.

"When are we meeting Aunt Dot and Grandmother? I know they've both called several times."

Jan stood up abruptly, her fist slamming the table. Her voice stern, she locked eyes with me, the intensity in her gaze unyielding.

"I knew about you and chose to NEVER reveal your existence to my mother. I need you to promise me, right now, to keep this secret."

I was speechless. After five tense minutes, I finally met Jan's gaze. "If we aren't going to meet them, then it's time for us to leave."

Jan leaned back in her chair, the edge in her voice softening.

"Okay," she sighed, "I'll arrange to meet tomorrow."

Her behavior was baffling. I was aware of the phone calls to the house; why was she acting like this? I told her David and I needed a break so we were headed out – of the house – not out of town. Not yet. Not while there was a chance of meeting my grandmother.

"Mom, where are we going?"

"To the cemetery where my mom, your grandma, was laid to rest." I took one last shot at civility with Jan and asked if she would like to join us at the cemetery. After a sharp "No!" we loaded up and left.

Sweet kid that he is, David turned to me and said. "We have to take flowers! Yes, oodles of flowers. Aunt Jan said grandma's favorite color was pink."

At a florist near the cemetery, David helped pick out flowers for the mother I'd never met. I did everything I could to stop the tears from pouring out of my eyes.

Her plot was on top of a hill with a beautiful vista. I stood in silence for several moments as David cried. This was his first visit to any cemetery; he didn't know what to expect. We sat on the ground and talked to Donna for a half-hour.

When we left I was tempted to drive to my grandmother's, but we ended up heading back to Jan's instead. Aunt Jan had dinner ready, and we were told to wash up, sit and eat. And get ready to go to the track.

Back at the house, we were ready to turn in. On our way to the basement, I had to remember to duck to avoid smacking my head. It was dark and dank and smelled like old books. We got into our beds and both felt a chill. I flicked on a small desk lamp on an old wooden box and could see blankets all along the wall. As I took two down, I realized they were horse blankets. Maybe that was part of the smell. I lifted another and saw a number of large labeled boxes.

*Donna Switzerland. Donna Paris.*

David's whispered, "Aunt Jan is coming."

I put the horse blankets back and turned out the lamp. We sat silent in the dark, as we saw the light go on and off and heard my aunt creaking back up the stairs.

As tempted as I was, I didn't pry. It was not my house, and Aunt Jan had proven to be unpredictable; I didn't want to rock that boat. I slept fitfully imagining sporting awards, unique designer clothing labels, and heaps of gold watches, pictures of Donna laughing with friends, blushing as she received an award, zipping off in fancy cars with unknown boyfriends …

Morning came. Jan creaked down the stairs to announce her mother was still not ready to meet us.

"David, why are you standing against that wall? What happened to those blankets along the wall? Did you see anything, David?"

David shook his head no. "Nothing, Aunt Jan. I was just playing."

I felt sorry that he had to lie, but I understood he was protecting me.

We went upstairs and sat around the kitchen table, where my aunt shared more stories – even attempting to add humor to some.

"Your great-grandmother Annie worked as a waitress for thirty-five years at the Aristocrat in Vancouver. The boss would be off on Sunday mornings, and she would fill the restaurant. There wasn't a seat left in the house, and she fed everyone for free. The boss fired your grandmother when he found out.

"These customers were poor, and many were homeless. They had no money for food. It was a way to give back to the community. Three weeks passed, and her boss called and hired her back. He told her he had lost two-thirds of his business. Your grandmother agreed to go back, with a raise."

We headed to Langley to meet Aunt Dot. I had a travel brochure about Langley, and I read it aloud. "Famed for fine wineries and farmland, Langley is 37 kilometers southeast of Burnaby."

"It's the horse capital of British Columbia," Jan added.

"When was the last time you saw your sister?"

"Three years."

She was driving slowly as if to delay this meeting. My offer to drive was met with a scoff, and we arrived two hours later than planned. When Aunt Dot opened the door, I saw her face change from irritation at our tardiness to one of elation when she saw me. She stared as if she had seen a ghost.

"Diana, may I hug you?" She wrapped me in her arms then stood back and looked me in the eye. "Your resemblance to your mother is uncanny."

There was a world of difference between Jan and her sister. Dot exuded elegance and class. Her appearance was flawless and she had a gentle manner. In contrast, Aunt Jan was a simple country girl – always in jeans and a white shirt. She had the natural, barefaced look of a gardener.

Standing in the kitchen was another woman.

"Hi Diana, I'm Marty, short for Marlene. I'm your aunt's roommate. And this young man must be David."

"Marty, how long have you lived here?"

"A little over twelve years. We're both divorced, neither has children and we wanted to live in the country, and this house is perfect: great neighborhood, huge fenced yard and breathtaking gardens."

Dot interrupted, "Diana, let me give you the tour while Marty and Jan entertain David. She's had you all to herself for the past five days." The great room was full of watercolor paintings. A glass unit full of memorabilia stretched from one end of a wall to the other. One treasure caught my attention. It was a bronze sculpture on a marble base depicting two hands of varying sizes holding each other. I stared at it for such a long time that Dot took note.

"Is that your favorite piece on the shelves?"

"Oh, Dot, the hands! They are magnificent."

"I've been filling the cabinet with art and antiques for

years. Of all the art, you chose the only piece given to me by your mother. You must have it."

Back in the kitchen Dot and Jan resumed talking about my mom; Jan seemed displeased.

"I want to give you the hands art since you had nothing of your mother's, and I've had them for twenty-five years."

"Dot but I can't accept them. That's the only treasure you have of her!"

"Not if you count what's in the basement …," David muttered to me.

Hoping no one had heard him I changed the subject. No way did I want Aunt Jan to know we knew about the boxes in the basement. But how could we not? She stuck us down there like maybe she wanted us to find them? Out in the hallway I could hear her arguing with Dot about giving me anything. This was downright spooky.

The tour went to the deck; a long walkway was flanked by colorful flowers and lush native plants. It was like an artist's palette leading to the deck.

"The goldenrod brings sunshine. No matter the weather, the red columbine is full of butterflies and hummingbirds."

After dinner, we sat on the deck. Marty brought out coffee and chocolate cake – which Dot said was Mom's favorite. I liked Dot and Marty.

"Do you know you are the sole biological child?" asked Dot.

"No, not until now. I only knew grandmother had five children."

"In 1953, I had an arranged marriage. We were married for eighteen years and never had children. After enduring years of mental and physical abuse I finally got out. Marty got me through those tough times, and I found happiness again."

It was clear Marty was Dot's life partner, not a roommate.

Dot kept on … "I want you to know that you two are our legacy now that you've found us. Diana, you're the only biological granddaughter, and David is the only great-grand-son. You both need to know your family history, culture, and food. You are the sole heirs. David can carry on the legacy."

I was so comfortable with Dot and Marty that I wanted to stay and learn more about my mother but Jan was ready to go home, claiming Orland needed her.

Dot said, "I'll see you tomorrow."

Jan stiffened. "We won't be returning."

"I'd like to spend the day with my niece and great-nephew, so I'll come to you tomorrow since you've been taking up all of their time." The looks between the two sisters made it clear they were at odds.

Jan was quiet on the way back, I could feel her animosity towards her sister. I was careful choosing my words.

"Thank you for taking us to meet Dot and Marty."

Jan's voice was raspy and harsh when she announced, "We're going to your grandmother's house tomorrow after breakfast."

And we did. I drove; we were there in less than twenty minutes. A man in a white polo shirt and blue jeans was identified as Uncle Freddie who took care of grandmother and the house. From the outside, it looked like a haunted house from a comically scary movie. Jan walked straight to her mother in the kitchen. I stood back – after all, she was the matriarch. As she saw me for the first time, my grand-mother took a deep breath and sighed, "Oh, Donna." Every-one turned to stare at me; time seemed to stop. She called me to her side … David followed.

Grandmother took my hands in hers, squeezed them tightly, and proclaimed: "You are Donna's daughter."

A tour of the house was accompanied by an oral history.

"I was raised during the Great Depression, born during

harvest time in 1914 in Arran, Saskatchewan, Canada. I married Frank when I was fifteen and had five babies before I was twenty-five years old."

Back L to R, Grandmother, Ron, Freddie
Front L to R, Jan, Donna, Dot

In her bedroom was a picture of grandmother with her five young offspring. Her bed was a black metal frame, the thin mattress only about a half-inch thick. She said it reminded her of surviving the Great Depression.

*Why didn't her daughters buy her a decent bed? Didn't they care?* This was creepy. I wanted to leave. Then I heard David scream.

I found him with Great Uncle Freddie – and Freddie was dressed as a samurai warrior. He was brandishing two swords and spoke to me in Japanese. One sword was large, the other smaller. Jan burst into the room. David was whimpering against the wall. I grabbed David and said to Freddie, "You're scaring him! Whatever it is you're doing. Stop!"

We rushed back to the kitchen; Aunt Dot had arrived. I needed to know the story behind Uncle Freddie. Clearly he was much more than my grandmother's groundskeeper. I wondered aloud if he was autistic.

"Freddie's brain is wired differently." That's all she said, then she handed me an envelope, whispering, "Take this, and don't tell the girls. Your mom was an angel. Be careful of Jan."

It was time to go. We hugged my grandmother and headed back to the car.

"How do you let them live like that?" I couldn't believe they'd let an old woman sleep on a rickety old metal cot, and Uncle Freddie seemed beyond weird.

Aunt Dot spoke up, "If we buy her anything, she donates it to the poor."

We all had dinner at a local restaurant. I was surprised to see my eccentric Uncle Freddie. This could be interesting. Grandmother told David she was happy we had come to Vancouver. There was good conversation and lots of laughter.

Aunt Dot seemed to read my mind, "We are family, even though we may not be what you expected."

I told her I had no expectations when I decided to visit Vancouver. After losing my parents early in life, I was looking for my roots. Family history goes far beyond names and dates; I wanted to be able to form connections … to help develop a strong sense of who I really am.

The family agreed we needed to get to know one another better and said they hoped we'd come again soon.

Back at Jan's house, I started to pack. I took the envelope my grandmother had given me earlier and opened it. Enclosed were scraps of paper with four handwritten poems, fifty dollars, and the Prayer of St. Francis of Assisi:

"It is not always what we seek but what we find, which proves our heart's desire and shows us God is kind."

Tears of joy rolled down my face. Before I knew it, the morning light awakened me.

I loaded the car by dawn and heard David watering the vegetable garden one last time. I wanted to catch the nine o'clock ferry. We said our goodbyes and headed out.

As we boarded I sensed a presence. I turned around and saw a man in the distance. He was tall and olive skinned

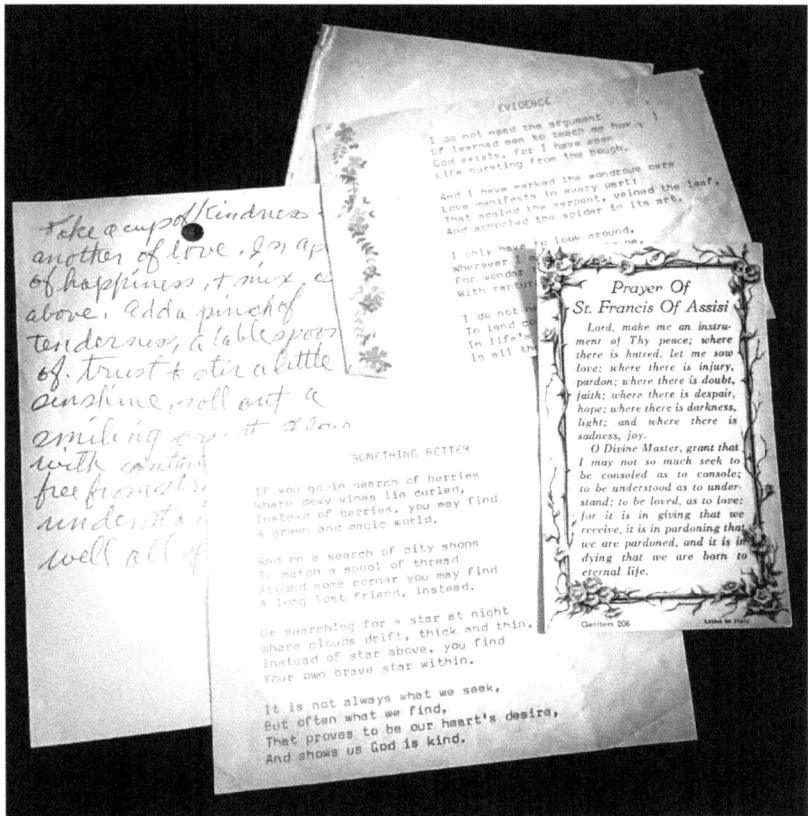

Grandmother's gift.

with dark hair and a mustache, and he was staring at us. His trench coat, boots and slouch hat did not suit the weather. Even David noticed. I felt increasingly vulnerable. After the bizarre antics of Uncle Freddie, I decided I was still spooked and ignored my gut as we took the drive south to Victoria.

As we passed logging trucks I speculated about Uncle Ron; we didn't get to meet him or his wife, Jeanne. He moved to Victoria Island at fourteen and was a logger for forty years. Grandmother said his job was hard, honest, and dangerous – and he loved it.

I caught myself looking in the rearview mirror. And something made me lock the doors. In Victoria we parked the car and decided to walk through Thunderbird Park. David ran to check out the totem poles, an amazing collection of indigenous artwork. Around the corner was the Royal British Columbia Museum where we explored a special exhibit on Genghis Khan.

And there we saw the man who had been on the ferry. Was he following us?

Determined to make the most of the remaining holiday time we explored the area and indulged in an exceptional meal before returning to the States. I let the time get away from us and suddenly realized we had only forty-five minutes to catch the last ferry of the night. We ran to the car, but it was too late; the gates were locked. The next ferry to Seattle boarded at six AM and left at seven.

My first thought was to look for a hotel, but there was a special event in town. All the hotels were full. Stalling for time, I took David for ice cream. We went to a movie that offered 9:30 PM and midnight showings of *True Lies*. We bought tickets and stayed for both. When we stepped out at 2:30 AM, cars were lining up for the 3:30 AM ferry. We boarded and dozed in the car.

I wasn't asleep twenty minutes before a guy started knocking on the window. I freaked out when I realized it was the same man David and I had seen earlier in the day. This time, the man was alone. He was trying to tell me something.

"Lady, roll down your window."

"No!"

He reached into his pocket and took out his wallet, displaying a badge: Police Detective Alexander. "Madam, your tire is flat. Let me take care of it."

I rolled the window down enough to ask why he was following us. I thought his answer plausible, if a bit flimsy:

"It's rare to see an American woman traveling alone with a young man in this part of Canada. I noticed another man beside me who was following you, and I thought it best to be sure you made the ferry last night," he explained.

"Oh. Thank you for the concern."

He put the spare tire on in time before we boarded the ferry. I was relieved this man had come to our rescue, but concerned someone else had been following us, too. While we ate breakfast the detective stopped by our table.

"Madam, may I ask a question?"

"Yes, of course."

"Why are you visiting Canada?"

This guy was nosy, so I answered vaguely. "My mother was Canadian and we've never met that side of the family."

"I hope you return soon. Stay safe, and look after that young man."

As we parted ways, I could sense him close behind us. Even when we boarded the plane in Seattle, my instincts were on high alert but I chalked it up to watching too many crime dramas and settled into reviewing the events of our trip.

At first, it all seemed strange, finding a family who knew nothing about you for the last thirty-eight years. Could it develop into a normal family relationship? What was the rush? I no longer felt compelled to seek answers to all the questions about them.

I had found them; it was time to make new memories.

# Chapter 7
## *Montefiore Club*

Everything happened fast back in Florida. I took my old job back as administrative assistant for the regional manager of the jewelry store. The hours were good – Monday through Friday, 9 AM to 5 PM – more time for David and me. I'd miss the travel benefits of Continental, but it was best for us in the long run.

I kept in touch with Vancouver and the conversation always changed when I had questions about Donna.

I maintained contact with Mort Shulman and in the spring of 1996, he invited David and me to Montreal for a long weekend. I accepted.

"I have a wonderful surprise for you."

After all I already knew – or suspected – how could this guy possibly surprise me?

"An old friend of your mother's will be joining us for dinner. Donna lived with her while attending university."

I asked for a name and number and Mort stalled.

Two weeks later, I received a phone call from Adele Wiseman, the gal we were set to have dinner in Montreal. Mort had filled her in about the purpose of the meeting, and she wanted to talk to me first.

"I never asked Donna questions, but she always kept a baby picture on her dresser. I was told it was a close relative."

On the flight I told David to try to think of Mort as a grandfather.

Mort and Andrée's apartment was first class; a doorman led us to the penthouse. Mort gave me a bear hug and turned to David to shake his hand. Andrée kissed us on both cheeks. She couldn't help noticing I was "a clone" of my mother.

Dinner was delicious and the conversation pleasant. We talked about our Vancouver visit. Mort seemed uneasy, tense. After dinner, David excused himself to relax with a book and Mort retold the story of taking Donna and the baby – me – across the border.

"What else did you do for my mother?" Andrée sighed and rolled her eyes. I didn't care. I was a little tired of this guy's macho crap.

I asked the big questions. "Are you my father? Did you have an affair with my mother? Do you know who my biological father is?"

Andrée couldn't help but interrupt. "Oh, Mort fell in love with Donna while helping to place her baby, but he isn't your father. She shut him down every time he'd try her. She had an idea of the people he did business with, and besides, he was a married man. Your mother had goals and no time for nonsense."

The next day we left early to explore the city while Mort and Andrée worked. Dinner reservations were at five at the infamous Montefiore Club.

Inside the three-story Victorian Greystone I felt like I was in a scene from *The Godfather*. The decor was fancy – the linen-leather-crystal chandelier kind of fancy. In its heyday, the club was a plush hangout for men to smoke cigars and play cards. When Mort saw Adele and Scarlett Wiseman approaching, I turned. Adele took one look at me and fainted. Mort hadn't told her I would be there. She regained her composure but kept calling me Donna as she stared at me the entire time.

Adele said I was brave; she admired my determination and

courage. She talked fondly of Mom, and how unbelievable my story was. I played it cool and blamed it all on Mort.

"Did Mort tell you about my daughter, Scarlett? She was adopted as a newborn, too."

"No, he didn't."

Did Mort "help" Adele, too? There was body language between them … *Hmmm*.

Though they had spoken on the phone off and on over the years, it had been three decades since they'd seen each other.

She got emotional, tearful even. I tried to make her comfortable. We talked about my career and David's upcoming bar mitzvah. Scarlett told me about her television career and hopes of a movie role. She said my mother taught her how to ski when she was seven; I was envious.

After dinner, Mort told Adele I would be unavailable during the rest of my stay; he didn't seem to want questions when Andrée was around.

We said goodbyes, and I exchanged information with Scarlett, I hoped she'd stay in touch. After a long day, we were exhausted and turned in as soon as we politely could.

I never saw Adele and Scarlett again during our visit. Mort was a control freak, and some people were afraid of him. I wasn't, and neither was my mother.

Mort's synagogue was close by, and he walked David and me to services the next morning. On the way back we passed McGill University, where Mom went to college. Since Andrée wasn't around, he talked freely about Mom.

"Donna was classy and stylish. She worked two jobs – three if she had time – and attended classes. Every month she mailed a check to your grandmother in Vancouver."

"She bought gifts for you and I'd pass them to Manny when he came to Montreal. They had to be small; Ethel would have been upset if she knew who bought them."

By the tone of his voice, I could tell Mort cared for Mom.

Back at his place, his daughter Emma and her boyfriend Grey had arrived for a late lunch.

"Emma, do you remember Manny Hochberg's daughter Diana?"

"No, but I remember her father, Manny."

"Emma, what do you remember about my dad?"

"He handed me twenty dollars, and I thought it was play money. He called me candy ass." Emma laughed.

When Emma asked why I was visiting, I told her like it was … well, I added some tact.

"The Hochberg family adopted me; your dad knew my mother."

She had an awkward expression on her face. "Of course, he knew her. Did he tell you what her name was?"

Mort spoke up, fumbling for words as he wiped sweat from his forehead. "Emma, do you remember Donna? She worked for me as my bookkeeper a long time ago."

"Dad, you had so many."

I could feel the tension.

I told Emma I was never adopted and wasn't born in New York City. That I was looking for the truth about my identity, and it had turned into a full-time job.

Mort kept talking about my trip to Vancouver. He asked if I'd told him everything. I shared photos my aunt gave me. It irritated him that I'd been there two days and hadn't shown them before. I told him I waited for the right moment.

"Diana, you know your mom worked for me. And later, so did your aunt, Jan. She was a user and preyed on Donna. After your mom's disappearance, I mean after she passed away…"

"Mort! What happened?"

He sighed. "I was on the phone with Donna when she died. She said she was in a Vancouver hospital and would be out in a day or two, and ten minutes later, she was gone" —

he snapped his fingers – "just like that. I couldn't believe it. I told Janet I'd pay for everything, the funeral, her plane ticket … but Janet was adamant; she wasn't going. She was in complete denial and ended up staying with me for ten months before going back to Vancouver."

Not for the first time, I was speechless. I went to bed and left for the airport the next day. I was overwhelmed with this new information about my mother and her mysterious death. David and I sat in silence on the way home. I think we both had a lot on our minds.

I needed time to process everything.

Again.

# Chapter 8
## *Have You Seen Her Father?*

Over the next few years I thought a lot about Donna and my Vancouver relatives. Though we had been somewhat welcomed (I couldn't shake the basement memories), it still wasn't enough. I wanted to know what happened to my mother. Not once had I felt I was being told the whole truth.

I thought about my dad, Manny, too. After twenty-six years of marriage, he lost his wife to cancer and became a single parent balancing work and well, me. He was forced out of his factory in Brooklyn and had to set up in a new facility in 1967. That's when I started tagging along on his business trips.

As it happens, life moved on after Ethel and Donna passed. Manny never remarried, Mort Shulman continued as a traveling merchant while managing Dad's Montreal subsidiary of Canada specializing in metal fabrication.

I pondered the unknown, afraid of the answers. Was it true Mom never told her sisters or best friend about her pregnancy? She told no one besides Doris Langerak, a mutual friend of Donna, Dot and Janet? How could they not have known if Doris did? I can't imagine Mom's thinking. Was this for her good or mine?

David and I went back to Vancouver in July of '97. We stayed with Dot and Marty, and I treated us to a sports car for the weekend. Everyone had been nice on our last trip …

and we had kept in touch; going to Vancouver felt like going home. It was late evening when we arrived. Marty and Dot wished us a good night's sleep; we'd catch up in the morning.

I smelled coffee and joined Dot in the kitchen. We made morning small talk. She had booked a 10 o'clock tee-off time for David, meanwhile we would go shopping, get manicures, and have lunch. I was thankful we could enjoy a girl's day.

I had made an appointment with a Vancouver reporter while I was there in hopes of telling my story and finding out about my birth father. During lunch, I reminded Dot about the interview on Thursday.

"We don't need reporters. You should cancel."

"Why would I cancel? The experience of meeting all of you has been a step forward for me. The reporter thought telling the story might help draw out clues about my biological father."

Aunt Dot's second thoughts about an article made her anxious. I changed the subject and left it alone.

The next morning Dot and Marty went with us to meet the reporter. We were early – maybe too early – it gave Jan time to backtrack.

"Do you have to do this, Diana? You know who we are now, we're family."

It was 9 AM; our appointment was in an hour. The part of me that couldn't forget the basement and the "Donna Boxes" wasn't even surprised when Jan announced she wouldn't allow photos or answer questions. Fine. Whatever.

When Dot answered the door for the reporter from *The Province*, I didn't recognize them.

"Where's Gordon?"

"He was called out on another assignment. Most of your story is written in the letters between you and Mr. Clark already." He had a point; Gordon and I had corresponded for months.

We posed us for pictures, and the reporter asked questions. Aunt Jan refused to be photographed; it was just David and me.

After the interview was over we drove to Stanley Park – one of Mom's favorite places. I could see why. There were scenic paths, a nature center, flower gardens, and an aquarium. David and I took it all in, Jan's rudeness faded.

We picked up Jan on the way to Ronnie and Jeanne's the next morning. Ron was humorous and good-natured; Jeanne was soft-spoken. Like everyone else, Ronnie couldn't get over how much I looked like Donna.

We got to know each another over lunch. Jeanne had never met or heard of my mother until the week before. That struck me as odd, but this was not the time for questions. Afterwards we left for the airport and caught the red-eye from Vancouver to Clearwater. I called Gordon Clark about the article; I was told it was set to run in *The Province* newspaper, Monday, July 28, 1997.

I'd been in Clearwater a few days when a loud BANG woke me up from a jet lag coma. A blown transformer left my condominium complex in complete darkness with no A/C. It was as hot as Hades. Outside it was a record-breaking 102 degrees. Four steaming hours later the power clicked on, and my answering machine showed five new messages.

The first was Aunt Jan screeching into the phone. "How could you have done this to my family and me?"

Aunt Dot's said the newspaper article about us ran as a full page with the headline: 'Have You Seen Her Father?' and "Call me as soon as you get this, Diana."

The last two messages were from Mort Shulman. He was stuttering and dead serious. "Diana, we need to talk."

I was very much awake now. I went online and found the article.

I read it three times, shaking my head. I wanted to read

it objectively, you know, as someone not knowing Donna's story – my story. It made me feel ashamed and embarrassed because she was my mother. The article included a photo of David and me.

I called the paper and asked to speak to Gordon Clark. The front desk transferred the call and Clark answered.

After I identified myself, I told Mr. Clark that his article had caused a bit of a stir in my family.

So as not to burn a bridge, I said the article was well written, I was glad he'd mentioned Doris Langerak, and I hoped it would be helpful.

Then I hung up.

# Chapter 9
## *"We Can't Run That!"*

Lily Grouix and Donna Koloski at the English Bay Bathhouse, August 1953,
photographed by Stuart Davis, article written by Gordon Clark.
Photo courtesy of *The Province Postmedia*.

Staff photo by Stuart Davis

Ed Cosgrove shows censored photo of Vancouver's first bikinied beauty.

# Media covered up bikini's B.C. debut

**By Gordon Clark**
Vancouver Reporter

It'll be 50 years next month since the bikini made its big splash at a Paris fashion show.

But it would take another six years — and an immodest young fashion model named Donna Kolosky — for the itsy-bitsy bathing suit to wash up in Vancouver and on to the front page of The Province.

Ed Cosgrove, 69 and a BCTV reporter until last January, was a 27-year-old Province photo-journalist on Aug. 9, 1953, when he spotted the city's first bikini.

Cosgrove's memory was twigged by a recent magazine article on the suit — named after a U.S. atomic-bomb test site at Bikini atoll — that recalled its explosive effect.

It reminded him of that summer 46 years ago when Elizabeth II was crowned Queen, a New Zealand bee-keeper and his Nepalese guide conquered Everest and the Rosenbergs were electrocuted as Soviet spies.

"I was out on patrol and I noticed a big crowd on the English Bay bathhouse," said Cosgrove. "These guys had big smiles and this girl was enjoying all the attention."

Cosgrove, who'd made the front page a day earlier by saving two drowning men, snapped several photos, interviewed 18-year-old Kolosky and her pal Doris Langerak, 20, and rushed to the newsroom.

"I just got a picture of the first bikini in Vancouver," he exclaimed.

Editors then were as nervous and as unpredictable as today.

"Managing editor Bill Forst and city editor Gordie McCallum had a little huddle," Cosgrove recalled. "They said: 'We can't run that! We'll have people phoning complaints.'"

In October of 1997, a large envelope arrived from Canada with no return address. Inside was a copy of the front page of *The Province* dated June, 1966. At the top of the fold was a story by Gordon Clark accompanied by a photograph by Stuart Davis. On the left side the caption read, "Ed Cosgrove shows a censored photo of Vancouver's first bikinied beauty." The article's title was, "Media covered up bikini's British Columbia debut." A sticky note with an arrow pointed to a picture I'd never seen. It was a striking photo of my mother in a bikini.

I shook my head and wondered for the millionth time:
*Why had it taken all these years for me to know about this?*
I sat for a long time reading and staring.

*"The twenty-seven-year-old photojournalist took the photo on August 9, 1953. Cosgrove had just made the front page the day before and felt his career was on the rise."*
*"There was a huge crowd by the English Bay Bathhouse,"* wrote Cosgrove. *"Lots of smiles and cameras. Here comes Donna, strolling down the beach wearing nothing but an itsy-bitsy teeny-weenie polka-dot bikini from Paris."*

He interviewed Donna and had her sign photo release papers. She was with a friend named Doris Langerak. Cosgrove wrote, "Doris was a few years older, and I didn't include her in the photographs." He chose another woman, Lily Grouix, for a second shot – Lily in a one-piece and Donna in that revealing bikini.

"I just got a picture of the first bikini in Vancouver, he explained. Editors then were as nervous and unpredictable as today. Cosgrove recalled Managing Editor Bill Forst and City Editor Gordon McCallum agreeing, 'We can't run that! We'll have people phoning in complaints,' by Gordon Clark, Vancouver reporter, staff photo by Stuart Davis."

The woman pictured was vibrant and confident, full of power and self-assurance.

Cosgrove described her as "poised and attractive." She

walked, spoke, and stood in a gentle, methodical, and determined manner. She was a pleasant, self-assured lady. This woman believed in herself. She reminded me of Audrey Hepburn, who was confident and self-assured.

If I'd been determined before, nothing was going to stop me from learning everything about my mother now.

I called the Vancouver newspaper and asked to speak with either Ed Cosgrove or Gordon Clark. I hadn't heard from Gordon since August. I reminded him that I had reached out to him, not the other way around; he knew what I had been through. For me, Gordon Clark was a vital link to Vancouver.

After a long game of phone tag, Clark finally reached me. I told him I was calling to check on the 1953 newspaper article. Without answering, he started asking me questions and changed the context of the conversation.

"When will you be back in Vancouver? I want to interview you."

"Not until next summer."

"Let me research. I'll pass on anything I find."

He had helped in the beginning when I was naive about the press; I hoped he could do so again. If I had to go on this journey I hoped to develop reliable friends and contacts along the way. He seemed like a candidate.

Several more weeks passed before I received a call from an apologetic Ed Cosgrove.

"I'm embarrassed not to have gotten back to you sooner."

"It's no problem; I've been busy, too."

"I'm flattered you reached out to me. Your story is incredible. I remember your mother vividly. She was beautiful and seemed surrounded by an aura white and bright; the closer you were, the stronger the effect. I can still see her strolling along the shore wearing the bikini. It was a beautiful summer day … a pleasant 70 degrees out, and there was a crowd. And all eyes were on her. There were men in business suits at the beach – men who didn't look or dress like locals – men who were clearly out of place. I remember wondering why they were there.

"The month before, Hollywood had been in town to photograph Marilyn Monroe. Maybe Donna wanted to be the next hot starlet – she had all the right stuff – all she needed was a break. Everything would have been different if the newspaper had run those pictures. She would have been the first woman photographed in a bikini in North America. She would have made a name for all of us, but the Vancouver newspapers were not ready for the hype it would have caused."

As the conversation ended he said he'd be in Vancouver the next week and would go by *The Province* make copies from the originals for me.

"That would be great, Ed! Thanks."

The holidays passed with no mail from Gordon Clark. But on New Year's Day, the phone rang: it was Ed.

"I mailed pictures to you last week; they should be there any day. I researched photographs I've cataloged through the years and found some I saved but never turned in. Several were shots of your mother talking with a man who appeared to be from out of town. I didn't mail those; I want more info before I do. I'm intrigued by the story of your mother. Do you know how she died?"

I told him what I knew, and he got quiet. He asked me to call him when the pictures came. When they did, I was astounded by my mother's beauty. I wondered who the other people were. I called to thank Ed; we promised to stay in touch.

It was the afternoon of May 5, 1999, when my plane touched down in Vancouver. Dot and Marty were expecting me for dinner. It had been four months since Ed Cosgrove sent the clippings and pictures. During our correspondence he'd talked about my mother as if they were friends, and I was eager to meet him.

As soon as Dot opened the door I was greeted with a big smile and a bigger hug, as if it were the first time we'd met. A great smell wafted through the foyer; Dot had been cooking Ukrainian food all day. They wanted me to experience a taste of my heritage. Dot made Marty's favorite dessert – crisp pastries filled with rum. I marveled at the meal.

We moved to the patio and the conversation became personal.

"We're always glad to have you, but I have to wonder … what are you looking for? Aren't you satisfied with what you know?"

I paused before I answered Dot. "Was Mom in good health before she left for New York City? Why was she in Vancouver?"

"Your mother and I were close; I assumed she would tell us all what was going on before going to New York."

"Well, what was her job?"

For the next ten seconds, all was silent.

"Donna was a bookkeeper. She modeled on the side. That was all she let on. She was a very private person."

"Aunt Dot, I have a meeting with Ed Cosgrove."

"When?"

"I was planning on meeting him while you were at work." Suddenly, Dot was enraged and demanded I "drop it and walk away now."

I walked away from her, but no way was I walking away from my appointment.

The next day I called Ed Cosgrove at home. On the third ring, a man answered. It was Pete. Ed had mentioned Pete several times over the phone, they were friends from Port Moody.

"Cosgrove residence, can I help you?"

"Yes, I'm looking for Mr. Cosgrove."

There was a pause. "May I please take your number? I'm afraid I can't talk now." His tone was somber.

I identified myself. "Ed and I have an appointment.

"I'm sorry to inform you over the phone, but Ed died Sunday, May 2nd, after a long illness. I'll call with details when I can. I'm sorry, Diana. Ed spoke highly of you."

I couldn't believe my ears. The man I'd been counting on to help me – the man I'd been writing to and calling … the man who had supplied vital clues to the mystery was … dead?

Stunned, I managed to summon my manners and ask if there was anything I could do.

"Nothing at the moment."

I hung up and began to process this disturbing information.

I should have asked the hospital's name. Why had I waited so long? I should have insisted on the other photos of my mother immediately.

Pete called back Saturday at noon with details about a celebration of life for Ed. I thanked him for the info and asked for an address. The least I could do was send condolences. There was no way I could attend. I had plans with the family, then a plane to catch.

Grandmother, Tom, and my aunts joined me for dinner in town.

"Why didn't you bring David this trip?"

"I had business in Vancouver and, anyway, he had plans."

"What type of business?" I couldn't believe Jan was asking me this. I told her I had a meeting with Ed. No one seemed to realize how intent I was on finding out more about Mom.

I whipped around to face her, my mouth set, my voice stern. "Remember Ed Cosgrove, the man who took the bikini photos of my mother? He knew things about my mother. We've been corresponding for months. I was supposed to meet him. HE's the business I'm here about. Well, he WAS. Today I found out he died last Sunday after a long illness."

Clearly irritated, Jan spoke. "I don't understand why you were talking to him? Do you think I wasn't telling you the truth?"

"I don't know what to think! Were you telling the truth? Are you? Do you think you are protecting me? Your version of things sounds like fantasy. Is there any truth to them? Why have you never visited my mother's grave? Were you upset with her? Did you quarrel?"

So much for a special night with family; Jan shifted gears. "Your mother is no longer alive. Is there anything else you need to know?"

Dot tried to change subjects, bringing up her watercolors and a new community workshop she was starting. Her enthusiasm somehow overcame the quarrelsome tone of before, and she took control of the conversation. I was glad and let it slide. There was nothing to be gained by ending my time here with an argument.

I couldn't wait to get back to Florida. I missed David, who had stayed with Kathy and her family. When I got to her house, there he was, holding a sign that read:

*Happy Mother's Day!*

# Chapter 10
## *Who Is Doris Langerak?*

The company I worked for downsized and my regional manager's assistant position was eliminated, but I landed a new job as assistant manager at one of the top fine jewelry stores. I was settling into my new role when I discovered a missed voicemail from Gordon Clark, the reporter from *The Province*. He said I needed to call him to discuss Doris Langerak. He was excited to have located her almost two years after the newspaper article was published and had just spoken to her in Fort Lauderdale. Doris confirmed she'd worked as a dancer at the Penthouse, was a few years older than my mother, and she had snuck Donna into the club every night. She said the club was notorious for gambling, smuggling, and bootlegging – which was not news to me. Doris named several specific men at the club, adding Donna didn't want to get involved because she said they were a serious crime family, and "You couldn't just tell these men you were pregnant."

I was beginning to understand why Mom might have left for Montreal. Aunt Jan mentioned Mom dating an Italian from the West End, whose brother was known to enjoy gambling. She said they were the Petrillo brothers, who were good friends with the Fillipone brothers.

Mr. Clark offered to try to find those men. I thanked him but said I thought I had sufficient information.

Doris mentioned plans to visit Vancouver to finish the interview. I asked Mr. Clark to contact me after their meeting. I then told Gordon Clark that I had found out I was not the first baby Mort Shulman had sold.

That night I didn't sleep well. It took me a day or two to digest everything. I thought it over and decided I needed to get to Fort Lauderdale before Doris left for Vancouver. I wanted to see Doris Langerak face-to-face, to look her in the eyes. I kept calling until I reached her.

"Diana, I am still shocked I am speaking with Donna's daughter."

She acted as if she didn't know who Mort was.

I was persistent about Doris's schedule and meeting her in person.

"Diana, for the next ten days, I'll be working. Then I leave for holiday to Vancouver. I was great friends with your Aunt Dot and saw Jan, but we didn't hang out."

"May I ask a few questions?"

"Sure, go ahead."

"When did you leave Montreal? And where did you go after you left?"

"I lived in Mexico for many years and have been in Florida for the past three. I can change my schedule this week to meet you. I'm off on Tuesday."

"Great! Let's meet on Tuesday."

Before the call ended, I asked a few more questions. "Where do you work?"

There was no response; it was dead air.

I tried again. "Do you remember when you and Mom left Vancouver?"

"I believe we left late in the autumn after harvest."

"Did you take the bus, train, drive, or fly?"

"Your aunt Dot took us to the airport."

When I asked if she could remember any activities in

which she and my mother had taken part, Doris seemed concerned about reliving the past after forty years. Her stories and dates seemed off. Either her memory was incorrect, or she was lying.

I must have changed my outfit four times before deciding on a red sundress and driving to Pompano Beach for lunch with Doris.

I had been preoccupied with work and neglected to write my usual list of inquiries so I took a notebook and a tape recorder. The crucial question I wanted answered was *why my mother left Vancouver in the first place.*

But other questions lingered ... *How did Mort Shulman come to be Doris's friend? Was she sure she didn't know my father's last name?*

I felt uneasy, as if I had a panic attack. My heart started to race so fast I couldn't breathe. I promised myself I'd finish this and discover the truth. I closed my eyes, took a deep breath, and pictured myself with David. Memories of happy times with my son always calmed me down.

I got back into my car drove to Krista's Castle Resort Hotel in Boca Raton. The views were spectacular.

When I parked, I noticed a woman staring at me. The woman was about five-eight with light brown hair, black pants, and gold jewelry. She wore oversized designer sunglasses. It was Doris.

We went into the dining room where and took a quiet table with a view of the ocean. Doris was a nervous wreck from the moment we met. She was clumsy during lunch, and her voice became coarser when she mentioned my mother.

"Diana, we are being watched."

Startled, I glanced around.

"Who would care about me being with Donna's daughter?" Doris asked.

When I asked her about the article, she lied to me.

"Doris, what did you find wrong with the article?"

"Donna never dated Mort, and this is his fantasy," she said. "I never knew your mother was pregnant back then. Mort is a good man who assisted us."

She took a brief break to go to the restroom. When she returned, I asked her if she recalled when they moved to Montreal.

"As I told you when you called the other day and asked if it was the fall of 1955. I told you I couldn't remember the precise date or year. I'd worked at Vancouver's The Penthouse Nightclub since 1950 and used to sneak your mother in all the time. In the 1950s, it was known as a bottle club. The Filippones helped to promote jazz and comedy. Sammy Davis Jr. and Louis Armstrong performed at the club. We were all pals, and Gary Cooper and Errol Flynn visited the club. The Filippone brothers were Joe, Mickey, Jimmy, and Ross Filippone."

Doris informed me that a robber had murdered Joe in 1983, and Mickey had also passed.

"I've already booked lunch with Ross and Jimmy. I'll ask about your mother while I'm in Vancouver," Doris said. The afternoon flew by, and she asked a strange question. "Does Mort know I'm with you today?"

"No, why would he?"

"I need to call him."

"What? Why?"

She whispered, "Diana, you are naive and don't understand."

"Then why don't you explain it to me? Wait a minute — is Mort involved in Montreal's underworld?" She never answered me but changed the conversation by telling me about leaving Montreal.

"I left in 1963, a lifetime ago, and I married and moved to Mexico. I hadn't seen your mother since she graduated from McGill University in 1959. I chose this hotel for today's lunch because I perform here in the lounge. I want you to understand that I have a stake in this hotel, and I am one of the three owners; the other two are tied to the Mafia. Diana, I ought to tell you that Mort has helped many women over the years, including me."

It was getting late, so we took photos and stepped out onto the patio, which overlooked the beach. When Doris turned to face me, her sunglasses fell down on her face. That's when I realized she was staring me down. "Are you satisfied? Will you quit searching now?"

"No. I'm just getting started."

"I can tell you are strong, like your mother."

Doris readjusted her sunglasses, so I couldn't see her reaction when her phone rang. "Diana, I must go."

"Is it possible for me to return tomorrow?"

"It would be pointless to return."

So, we went our separate ways. Doris embraced me and kissed me on the cheek.

"I'll be at the Penthouse next week."

But we both knew this would be our only meeting.

Carol Chycoski, a friend from Vancouver, sent a private message through Messenger that evening. Doris and her mother were photographed together at the Penthouse Nightclub in 1954. Her mother knew my mother.

# Chapter 11
## *A Killer Calls*

The sunrise was spectacular, and I woke up in a great mood, feeling positive about my new career path and the changes it was bringing. I felt I was exactly where I was supposed to be. I was promised a second raise and a promotion. David was happy. Our schedules were independently full: he was busy with sports a part-time job and a potential girlfriend. I had a fulfilling career, great friends and was active in our Jewish community. Everything was as it should be. I had a fantastic relationship with my birth family in Vancouver. Every letter from them closed with notes of endearment … 'wish you were here, miss you, we love you,' … making the miles between us seem not so far.

One evening, I was too tired for the kitchen routine so we ordered take-out and I was showered and in bed by ten. I was reading when the phone rang. I tried to ignore it. It was late; I wanted to sleep, not talk on the phone, but it kept ringing and finally I picked up, irritation in my voice.

"Hello … Hellooooo? … Is anyone there?"

"Hi, I'm looking for Diana Hochberg. Am I speaking to her?" It was a male voice.

As soon as I identified myself, the caller's tone became sinister.

"Stop searching for your father."

I was so stunned that I hung up. Not this again. I thought

I had reached a point where things like this would stop happening. It had been years (how many?) since I'd worried about my past.

Five minutes later, it rang again and I picked up.

"**Don't hang up**. I know what David looks like and where he goes to school."

"Who is this? Do I know you?"

"I'm the one who cleaned your house in Sarasota a few years back."

He was referring to the burglary of our home that terrorized us in '93. Our house had been ransacked – jewelry, artwork, extensive adoption research papers, photo clippings – everything was gone without a trace. The invasion had left us feeling vulnerable and caused an unnerving chaos in our tranquil neighborhood. I'm sure they were delighted when we moved to Clearwater.

The voice wasn't finished. "That was a small taste of the trouble I can cause you. And don't get any ideas about calling your old family or the cops. I can make you and anyone you care about disappear – and I will if I find out you've discussed this conversation."

Shivers shook me as I hung up. I was scared out of my wits. I thought of my future and my son's. It had been years since the Sarasota burglary and suddenly this man was calling and threatening harm to my son, his friends and my Vancouver family? What had stirred this up again?

In the days that followed I tried to remain calm for David's sake, but my mind wouldn't stop. I had spoken to a killer and I was terrified. His became "The Killer Voice" in my mind.

Months passed and keeping everything inside was making me physically ill. I felt crazy. I wasn't sleeping well. I was paranoid. I trusted no one, believed no one.

Running errands one day, I swore I heard footsteps behind

me. I was too afraid to turn around and look. As the footsteps seemed to grow louder, I sped up.

That's the day I had a full-blown panic attack that sent me to the emergency room. I wanted something – anything – to make this stop. After the ER doctor ruled out a heart attack and asked some questions, he gave me a quick fix but refused to write a prescription. Instead he recommended "seeing a counselor or participating in group therapy."

It made sense; I had allowed *The Killer Voice* to take over my spirit. Could this be why the letters from Canada had stopped coming? My intuition told me why the warmth between Canada and me had ceased. It's not a stretch to believe that my family had received the same frightening phone call. They loved David and me and would do anything for us. There was collateral damage that I had not anticipated. As a result, I knew I had lost my biological family that night to the man with a killer's voice. As long as I kept quiet and went about my business, David was safe. Everyone was safe.

I made up my mind to keep quiet. I'd go off the grid and live my new life in Clearwater. Calmness came over me. I trusted myself for the first time in months. It was time to put aside the worries and live the life we had built in Clearwater.

The killer's voice had won. For now.

# Chapter 12
## *More Lies*

Three years after the call, I flew to Montreal for a weekend. I thought about contacting Mort Shulman – this time I would be in control.

I checked into a hotel five minutes from McGill University, my mother's alma mater. As I explored the city over the next couple of days I fell in love the way Mom must have. Each district had its own personality. I imagined Donna in a pink couture designer outfit and fine jewelry in the artsy Ville-Marie district.

I stopped at several churches. I talked to a priest about the plight of a pregnant single woman in the 1950s in Montreal. He was brutally honest about the secrecy and what the young girls and women went through. It was heart wrenching.

Mort called so many times begging me to meet him that I finally agreed. He wanted to set things right and offered to sign any paperwork needed to help gain Canadian citizenship.

As time passed, the threat that had suppressed my search had morphed into a rage – I wanted to know every detail about Donna.

# Chapter 13
## *The Plaza Hotel 1967*

It wasn't until the spring of 2015, after I banged my head on the armoire, that I started having flashbacks of the events that affected my father's life. His wife, Ethel (my mother), was stricken with cancer in 1964 and died in March 1966. He was confronted with yet another challenge in his life.

Dad woke me early on Mother's Day in 1967. It had been slightly more than a year since Ethel's death. He came to my bedroom door and told me to get dressed for a trip to Manhattan.

But I had other plans. It was Michele's birthday and I was going to her party. I pouted and when he didn't notice, I stomped the floor.

He didn't notice that either.

He was chipper and whistling as he moved around the house.

"Why are we going to the city?"

"I have reservations for three for lunch at The Plaza Hotel."

"Three? Who else is coming?"

"Do you remember Mort Shulman from Canada?"

"Yes. The man with the big hat."

"That's the one. Well, we're having lunch with a friend of his. Her name is Donna. Remember the dress that came in the mail last week?"

"Yes."

"Well, she sent it."

Hmm. My young mind had concocted a scenario where Daddy had a girlfriend and the dress came from her. I thought he was trying to replace Mom, so I vowed to never wear it. Now that I understood differently, I loved the dress. It was yellow chiffon with white lace cuffs. It would look great with my white go-go boots. I had to hand it to Mort's lady friend Donna; she'd chosen the perfect dress. I'd admired it in "Teen Magazine." But how could she have known that?

I glanced at Dad's outfit and grinned; he'd always had an eye for style. His tailored suit was paired with a fedora and monogrammed handkerchief. He was keen.

Dad said I looked like my mother and called me his little princess. I knew I looked nothing like Ethel and gave him an inquisitive sideways glance. It had been more than a year since Mom had died. Manny was acting odd and nervous.

The Plaza Hotel sits across from Central Park and Fifth Avenue. The carpets were so thick in the lobby that you couldn't hear anything. Daddy said that's a part of old-world New York when conversations were meant to be private. The maître d' escorted us to our table. I sat next to Dad.

"What made you pick this place?"

Manny read the hotel's history from a brochure: The Plaza has hosted kings, presidents, and ambassadors as well as celebrities from the stage, screen, and sports have also stayed at the hotel. Mort told Dad that visiting New York City and seeing the Plaza Hotel was one of Donna's dreams, and he wanted to make it memorable for everyone.

We met in the Palm Court of the Plaza. As we waited, Dad told me about Mort's factory and that Donna was an office clerk and her sister, Jan, worked in the factory.

Time passed. Dad got quiet. He rubbed his palm across his brow and adjusted his jacket and tie. He was staring at the people coming through the door. When Dad did anything like this, I became more concerned. The longer we stayed, the more worried he seemed.

"Dad, she could phone you and leave a message at the Plaza, right?"

"She called Friday night to confirm our lunch."

I began to wonder if Donna would show at all. We'd waited for over an hour. Who does she think she is, hurting my father?

"Why is she taking so long? Can we leave and go to the park to see the animals? Please, Daddy. I can't wait any longer. Please?"

Looking back, I can't fathom the heartbreak my father must have experienced.

Donna never came and he eventually gave up waiting for her.

The plan was all set for a beautiful new beginning for us all. On Mother's Day, Donna was supposed to meet her daughter for the first time, but it never happened. The anticipated joyous celebration turned into a massive letdown. My father ordered my meal and continued to wait, stepping outside to smoke his stinky Cuban cigars. He couldn't eat and couldn't stop thinking about Donna. After I finished, Manny stood there, irritated. "C'mon honey, let's go to the zoo."

My father needed some time to collect himself. His emotions were getting the best of him, and I was concerned that he might lash out at the next person he saw. He tried to compose himself.

In the park people all around us were talking about Mickey Mantle's hits, including his 500th home run against Stu Miller. And The Yankees had won, 6-5. My father was a Yank's fan, and it seemed to brighten his day.

Even now, I don't know what happened that day. Donna was booked on Air Canada from Montreal to New York that morning. But no one knows for sure why she never appeared at The Plaza Hotel.

# Chapter 14
## *Seeking the Truth*

It was July 2015. I was organizing a ten-day fact-finding trip to Vancouver and had a list of contacts. One was Jim Millar, an old pal of Ed Cosgrove's. Jim was the curator of the Port Moody Station Museum. We'd talked by phone and he suggested contacting a local photographer who was also Ed's former neighbor – a reclusive widow who wasn't interested in talking to anyone new. He offered to serve as a liaison and asked for a list of questions.

I told Jim about Ed Cosgrove's demise and the intent of our failed meeting: I had wanted to know about his pictures of my mother from 1953 but Pete said a house fire destroyed them all.

Next, I called Port Moody Fire and Rescue. The dispatcher who answered was Beatrice. I asked for information about a fire call at Ed Cosgrove's home in May 1999.

"I don't see any records of a fire at that address on that date. Our system is old and incompatible with our computers. The old logbooks were archived years ago. Retrieving that information will be complicated. You can file a Freedom of Information application with the city and pay research costs. That decision is yours."

I told Beatrice I'd like to move forward and our call ended.

Next I reached out to Ethan Baron, a former columnist for *The Province*. On August 2, 2009, he'd written: "Mystery surrounds bikini model."

I was in North Carolina when the article broke. It included both Mom and a woman named Lily Grouix. Ethan not only connected me with Lily but also suggested I look for a Canadian reporter named John Fuller. I told Ethan I had a meeting with Aaron Chapman, a local historian and author of a book that focused on The Penthouse Nightclub. I was also meeting Aaron and Danny Filippone at the club.

Another lead came from a clipping of my mother modeling. During the '50s and '60s, she lived in Montreal. I have a copy of an ad for Browns Shoes dated April 1963. I looked up the company in Montreal and emailed Annie Cohen, the senior marketing manager for all Browns' shoe stores, with a copy of the photo.

Donna Kole Browns Shoes
Photo Credit Browns Shoes of Canada
Montreal, April 1963

Two weeks passed; I heard nothing; I followed up with another email. I received her reply. The modeling agency was no longer around … archives from fifty years ago are difficult to access. Meanwhile, I posted on our social media and will wait to see if we receive any bites. In the end, nothing came of this lead, other than more proof that my mother was a model-grade beauty.

The fact that I was the spitting image of Donna gave me no rights. I needed a paper trail. A Canadian relative could order documents, but since I legally had no family to ask, I had to be creative. I had my signature notarized at my bank. I knew the president and CEO personally, they had no reason to doubt the name I listed was my mother's.

On August 10, 2015, I had an email from "Gord" Clark; yes, he remembered Mom's story. No, he never knew Ed Cosgrove; he was gone when Clark arrived. Whatever photos Cosgrove took while on staff would be in the paper's archives. He was sorry he couldn't help.

I was speechless. I was amazed how little he recalled of our many conversations. I said I'd be in Vancouver August 16 and our conversation ended.

After Clark's last email, I decided to call the local police. Maybe I should speak to a detective? I wasn't sure if they could help me investigate something that happened fifty years ago.

The fact remained that I didn't know everything about the woman who had given birth to me. And I felt I had been thwarted at every attempt to find out.

# Chapter 15
## *The Hospital Records*

Months after my inquiry, I had a letter from Vancouver General Hospital.

*Coastal Health Record Services*          *August 11, 2015*
*Diana K. Hochberg*
*Clearwater, Florida USA*

*Dear Sir or Madam:*
*RE: KOLOSKI, Donna aka Camilla (Kolosky, Kole, Cole.)*
*Your request for information:*
*We acknowledge receipt of authorization to release all medical records for the above names.*

*We have conducted our usual thorough search, and find we have no record of this individual being treated as an inpatient or outpatient. She was never in our emergency room or any of our outpatient clinics. We regret we could not be of help to you in this matter.*
*Yours truly,*
*Maurice Kimble, CHIM*
*Certified in Health Information Management.*

There was no evidence Donna Koloski – or Kolosky, Kole, or Cole – had ever been admitted to Vancouver General or its emergency room.

A few days before I left for Canada, a Registration of Death came; survivors need it to apply for benefits or to settle an estate.

The information made no sense. It listed my mother's residence as Parker Street in North Burnaby, British Colombia. My mother never lived at that address; she lived in Montreal. My grandmother lived in the house on Parker Street and moved out in December 1965.

Neither my grandparents nor any of my mother's siblings signed the Registration of Death. Mort had told me Donna had flown to Vancouver from Montreal for a quick trip and was staying with Grandmother. The name on the Registration of Death was Joseph Gentile. *Who was this?* Every time I read it I had more questions. *Why was this strange name on the certificate?*

My mother supposedly flew back to Montreal on May 10, 1967 and continued to New York City on the morning of May 14, 1967. But she never showed in New York, no family member signed her Registration of Death, and there was no paperwork at Vancouver General Hospital.

It was another dead end.

## Chapter 16
### *Canadian Consulate 2015*

Months had passed since I'd mailed my application for dual US/Canadian citizenship to the Canadian Consulate in Miami. When I finally got a response, it came in the form of a rejection letter along with some alternative forms I could fill out, all of which required copies of documents I didn't have: proof of my father's citizenship; his certificate of birth or Canadian Citizenship; his status in the US: Alien Registration Card, US Visa, or US Naturalization Certificate.

A separate form titled "Application for Delayed Registration of Birth Abroad" required the completion of even more forms notarized with both sides of the notary seal accompanied by copies of my parents' marriage certificate, as well as a statement from a parent explaining why the birth registration didn't take place within two years of my birth.

I was flabbergasted.

Of course I didn't have this documentation! How could I confirm my own identity when I couldn't confirm those of my biological parents? It seemed my identity had been stripped away. All the years identifying as Diana Hochberg, daughter of Manny and Ethel Hochberg, seemed so simple now. Maybe I should have left it all alone. I was being thwarted at every turn trying to unravel the facts.

I called Henry Abbot, Mort's longtime attorney. A woman named Vivian answered. I gave my name and told her the reasons for my call. I asked her thoughts on Mort Shulman and mentioned I needed Henry's help. After a short wait and a few clicks on the line, we were all on a conference call. "Good afternoon, Mr. Abbott. I'm Diana Hochberg. My father was Manny Hochberg. He was in business with the Shulman family for over forty years."

"Of course I know who you are, Diana. Any chance you can come to Montreal for the weekend?"

"Not this weekend. As we speak I'm busy nailing down plans to be in Vancouver for the next two weeks. My plane leaves August 16."

Henry asked for details about Mort and seemed genuinely interested in helping me. So I told Mr. Abbott the basics: Mort was familiar with my adoption situation: he had known my biological mother ... that she (my mother) had passed away before she turned thirty ... I was on a quest for truth about my biological roots ... the whole spiel of my convoluted journey so far.

"And Mort led me to believe that he left official documents with proof of all of this with his attorney. And that has led me to you, Mr. Abbott. I'm under the impression that you are Mort's attorney. Would you please send me the papers? Mort signed documents claiming I was Donna's daughter, born in Montreal. My mother's name should be listed as Donna on the paperwork. Mort told me you would save a copy for me to use whenever I wanted it. He said he arranged everything when I was born. Please invoice me, I'll send immediate payment."

"We'll have to get back to you."

I assumed he needed time to properly gather the documents. So I thanked him and told him I looked forward to his call, bid goodbye to his wife/secretary, and hung up, satisfied that I had finally made a move in the right direction.

Later that night this email popped into my inbox:

*Subject: Important Notice Regarding Your Requests*
*Dear Diana,*
*I really do not want to get involved. Please do not bog us down in telephone calls or emails. We cannot help you. I do not mean to sound rude.*
*Henry Abbott*


I was astounded! What was with the hostile attitude all of a sudden? What could have possibly transpired to merit this? Only hours earlier, Henry and Vivian had sounded ecstatic to meet me, even extending an invitation for me to visit them in Montreal, and now they were treating me like a pesky telemarketer? I called again, hoping for clarity.

"Diana, back off, or I will report you to immigration and have you deported." Henry's tone was harsh and unwavering.

I tried to maintain my composure in the face of his threats.

"Henry, I've been living in the USA for the past sixty years."

He let out a sharp breath, frustration evident in his voice.

"Diana, you need to watch out. I can have you deported back to Canada."

"No, you can't."

"Watch me." Henry's voice was laced with determination.

I hung up and angrily composed an email bluntly stating I would cease all further contact.

I was perplexed. But I thought about Mort's behavior – and reputation. It had seemed shady at times. His outburst in Vegas had started this whole mystery tour. How did he and Henry Abbott ever cross paths? Henry was renowned for his integrity, with a 34-year career specializing in immigration counseling for prospective Canadian immigrants. He couldn't possibly have anything to hide. Or did he? Had he and Mort conspired in something that my search for the truth was in danger of uncovering?

An envelope from British Columbia Vital Statistics came the next day.

Inside was a Death Certificate.

*Deceased's name: Camilla Kolosky*
*Death Date: May 10, 1967*
*Location: Vancouver*
*Age: thirty years old*
*Born: British Columbia, Canada*

This was exasperating.

# Chapter 17
## *Hotel Blu, Vancouver, March 2015*

I'd stayed away from my mother's city for years, terrified by that threatening phone call – the "Killer's Voice" I'd called it. But I believed the stars had aligned, and I felt Donna pushing my search for the truth.

I landed in Vancouver on August 16, 2015, and took a car to Hotel Blu. When I could I'd made it a habit to treat myself to a comfortable home base while I was in town for research. Why not mix a little pleasure with work? Running down leads to my truth had turned into a busy pastime. So I chose Hotel Blu in downtown Vancouver for its easy access to everything I might need – dining, shopping, galleries, there was even a library ... but I wasn't up to exploring yet; I'd been on a red-eye flight all night and was exhausted. I guess the staff could tell; I was allowed to check in early and my room was upgraded to a deluxe suite with a king-sized bed. I fell fast asleep buried in a feathered tunnel of huge pillows, buttery-soft sheets, and a fluffy down comforter. I awoke revitalized and I took a walk to get a feel for my trendy home-away-from-home neighborhood before I started my day's call list.

First, I spoke with Gordon Clark at *The Province* to let him know I would be visiting Lily Grouix in Langley on August 20. (Lily was the other model in the swimsuit photos with Mom.) Lily and I were to meet face-to-face for the first time; we were both excited.

After Gordon Clark, I called Ethan Baron, the author of the '09 article that ran with the picture of Mom and Lily. I let Ethan know my meeting with Aaron Chapman at The Penthouse Nightclub was confirmed.

Then Aunt Jeanne and I spoke for a while, and Uncle Ron called later to set up a meeting for tomorrow. I also made several attempts to contact Aunt Jan, but all my calls went straight to voicemail. As planned, I spent most of the day on the phone, organizing my schedule.

The next day I was early to my 1 PM appointment at Jan's, so I decided to stop at what had once been my Grandmother's house. It had been fifteen years since I was here; the grounds and buildings were much improved. It took fifteen minutes to muster courage to ring the bell.

A petite woman answered. I introduced myself and told her this was my grandmother's former residence, pulling out an old photo as proof. She welcomed me without hesitation.

"I'm Gabrielle, from the South Pacific, and this is my son Jacob."

Gabrielle and I talked for two hours. I reminisced about my first visit to the property when it was Grandmother's. Gabrielle and her husband had searched for more than two years to find the legitimate owners after my grandparents' death.

I told her Uncle Tom took care of Grandmother until she passed, and after her death, he continued living here until he died in September 2010. I'd been estranged from my family for fifteen years.

She showed me around the newly renovated home, impressing me with the repairs she'd made; I'd always known it had potential. We took photos and she cried with me as I remembered my grandmother and uncle. I promised to try to make it back before leaving. Before I drove away, Jacob ran up and hugged me tightly. He muttered, "My mother is not a hugger; this enormous hug is from both of us." I waved goodbye as I drove away. It had been an emotional visit with many memories.

Turning into Aunt Jan's drive, I remembered the first time David and I came here. He was eleven years old. I remembered him working in the garden, the vegetables taller than he was. Now, it was overrun with weeds. I remembered being ushered to our sleeping quarters in the basement after being given a tour of the spacious four-bedroom home. I remembered the horse blankets and the boxes.

I rang the doorbell. Aunt Jeanne opened the front door.

"I don't think she'll let you in the house."

I passed her and saw Aunt Jan sitting at the table.

"It's your niece, Diana."

I knew Jan was sick with cancer and had been for a long time and that she had lost Orland in a tragic accident years ago. Feeling sorry for her sad state of affairs, I wasn't ready for her screams.

"Get out of my house; you're trespassing! If you don't, I'll call the police!"

"Aunt Jan? It's me, Diana! Call the police? What do you mean? I'm your niece, Diana!"

Jeanne was crying and pleading with me to go outside. I sat on the front steps.

"What happened to her?"

"I look after her during the day, and Dot comes in the evenings."

Clearly this was bad timing, but I pressed my luck.

"It's important that I talk to her. I've learned more about Mom."

"Jan doesn't want to talk about the past; after Orland died, she became meaner. I'm the executor of her will. You can have all her things after she passes."

"Can't I have them while I'm here? I've traveled 3250 miles."

"She keeps all your mother's items in a safe in her bedroom. When I ask questions about your mother's death and your father, she becomes hysterical and shuts down."

We went outside and Jeanne showed me where Uncle Tom was buried beside the vegetable garden. I was horrified to learn that he was buried in the yard and even more disturbed at the reason: Jan hadn't wanted to pay for his funeral or burial.

I couldn't take any more at the moment. I told Jeanne I'd see her and Uncle Ron over the weekend and left. As I drove away I pondered what I had learned over the years about Uncle "Tom" and his bizarre behavior as "Uncle Freddie," speaking Japanese and brandishing swords in samurai attire, and David screaming as I rushed to witness a scene that had yet to be explained. Uncle Tom/Freddie had some secrets of his own.

Thomas Frederick Koloski, also known as Tom or Freddie, had quite a muddled past. He was born on April 22, 1931, in New Westminster, British Columbia. In 1957, he traveled to Blaine, Washington, where he was granted federal naturalization on March 14, 1958, in Los Angeles.

He had a 1960 Brazilian visa for Rio de Janeiro, Brazil, that identified him as an unmarried chauffeur from Montevideo, Uruguay. When he died in 2010, I'd contacted the Vancouver police department and learned that a neighbor discovered his body in the house; he'd been dead for two weeks. An autopsy gave the cause of death as a heart attack.

I drove into the heart of Vancouver's downtown. The beaches are popular and it was teeming with tourists and tour buses. I parked near the seawall on the east side of the bay.

Donna and Diana at the same location 62 years apart. Left, photo
courtesy of *The Province Postmedia*; right, photo courtesy of a passerby.

English Bay Bathhouse and Stanley Park were both within
walking distance. Sunset Beach was my mother's favorite
beach; it was the scene of her iconic 1953 bikini photo.

I pulled out the photos of mother and compared the old
images to what I saw now. Not much had changed in the
remodel. It was the same down to the stairs and the ladies'
sign. I was taking pictures of myself when a passerby offered
to take some with my phone for a better angle. More than
once he made a comment about what an unusual place I'd
chosen for a photo shoot.

"My mother was in this exact spot on August 9, 1953." I
showed him the pictures.

I drove fast through Stanley Park. I'd been here with my
aunts and son years ago. The places we visited that day had

left indelible impressions. My aunts never stopped at the bathhouse back then; I would have remembered. Knowing what I knew now I wondered why. Surely they knew about the bikini photo. I wondered for the zillionth time what was going on.

At the hotel, I had made new friends. When I ran into Alex and Ryann they were chattering away about going to a nearby comedy show and talked me into taking a spare ticket. When the doorman looked at my ticket with a little surprise and wondered where it came from I mentioned Alex's name and was suddenly escorted past the long line and guided through a secret back elevator that led straight to the heart of the Comedy Club. I struck up a conversation with a woman in front of me, and she asked how I made it there before her and her friends. They were a lively bunch, invited me to join them, and adopted me for the evening. Her name was Eve Abrams. She was from Honolulu and had moved to Vancouver where she worked as the advertising account manager at *Vancouver Life Magazine.*

I began telling Eve about my mother. She asked to see the photo. I showed her the bikini picture in the hopes she could offer suggestions or ideas. She had some all right, and that night we became friends.

The next day I left Hotel Blu for Port Moody to meet Jim Millar, all the while wondering if I had to wait until Aunt Jan died to know what was in those boxes in the basement under the horse blankets.

*Donna in Paris.*

*Donna in Switzerland.*

# Chapter 18
## *City of the Arts*

I booked a hotel near Langley, and called Jim Millar to set up our meeting. He suggested noon at the Port Moody Railroad Museum. I went early and toured the town. Known for its charm, it has many small shops, galleries and restaurants. I met an artisan in one of the galleries who made gorgeous hand-painted scarves. I bought two – one for me, and one as a gift for Lily.

Jim had led me to believe his morning schedule was tight so I made sure to be there promptly at noon. But when I pulled in the lot Jim was waiting and offered a tour, assuring me there'd be plenty of time to talk about Ed Cosgrove later. I wondered what had happened to his tight schedule.

I shared my fascination with trains and recalled train trips from Grand Central to Midtown Manhattan along the scenic Hudson River with Jim adding commentary.

All of this was interesting, but I was here on a mission. So I interrupted.

"How is this related to my research on Ed Cosgrove?"

"Ed loved coming down to talk about trains. He lived in a quiet section of town near the SkyTrain. Back then, people regularly took it to Montreal."

The evasiveness in Jim's tone was clear. He wouldn't look me in the eye.

"Jim. I've traveled a long way and waited a long time to talk to you. Are you stalling?"

Jim took a deep breath and lowered his voice. "Diana I didn't want to say this over the phone but it may be best to approach the topic of Ed Cosgrove's pictures of your mother with caution. There's more to this than meets the eye. I think you're better off letting the situation be."

To say the least I was disappointed. I put off going to the fire station to tackle whatever red tape it was going to take to obtain records of the fire at Ed's that had destroyed his years of research. I had counted on the meeting with Jim being a success instead of the flop it had turned out to be. I drove back to my hotel feeling defeated.

Back in my room I gathered my wits and called John Grasty to discuss my grandmother's property. John had a good reputation as a Vancouver area realtor. I felt better after we talked. We had a productive call and arranged to meet that evening for dinner in the restaurant of my hotel. After my failed meeting with Jim Millar, I felt a tinge of optimism.

John and I met in the restaurant. We talked about grandmother's house, the property, the new owners and the renovation. I appreciated all the real estate tips he provided. It didn't hurt that he had a lovely English accent; it was a pleasure to hear him speak. I paid close attention to what he was saying. I had heard he was well connected in the community and could offer helpful leads.

As the evening progressed John ordered a bottle of wine.

"So you're searching for information on The Penthouse Nightclub and Ed Cosgrove's home, right?"

"Yes."

Like a detective, John took out a small black notepad and jotted names down. He looked up to say he was calling a guy named Vince Chessa. As they talked John jotted a name in his little black book. "What's that? Rizzuto? Got it. Pietro Rizzuto."

"How do you know Vince Chessa? Who is he exactly?"

"Vince Chessa Sr. worked at The Penthouse before his brother Sam owned and operated Black Top Cabs out of the same building as the nightclub. Black Top Cabs is still in operation. Given his connections, Vince likely knew about your mother."

I poured John another glass of wine. I felt like I was getting somewhere and I wanted more details.

"Diana, these conversations should be private."

Well, that was suggestive. I pretended not to hear. Wine glass in hand, he leaned back in his seat and studied me.

"Let me fill you in on the Rizzuto family. Pietro Rizzuto is well-known in Montreal. He was an Italian-Canadian politician who founded a construction company called Interstate Paving, Inc. He was appointed to the Senate of Canada by Pierre Trudeau in 1976."

"You should call Vince in Surrey, here's his number." He gave me a slip of paper.

"Do you think there was foul play in your mother's death?"

"Yes I do. And I'm curious and want the truth."

He seemed to be musing. "I've always been fascinated by my family history and roots. My father abandoned me when I was three. I applaud your bravery."

"John, Danny Filippone could be my half-brother."

"Ask Danny for photos. You might be interested in talking to Sean Holman, too. He's a well-known investigative journalist and documentary filmmaker in British Columbia. Here's his number."

We made small talk as the evening drew to a close, took photographs, hugged, and called it a night. I told John I'd keep him updated.

I felt good after dinner and drinks, and I slipped into the hot tub as I made a few calls to check out John's story about the Rizzuto's.

Vito Rizzuto was a distant relative of two Rizzuto family

lineages. Vito considered himself equal to the liberal senator, and Pietro had died three years before. Vito's family was much more esteemed in their hometown than in Pietro Rizzuto's hometown.

The next day was my sixtieth birthday and also the day I was to meet Lily Grouix for the first time. As I parked my car and headed toward her apartment building I heard a high-pitched squeal.

"Diana!"

Out on the balcony, there was tiny Lily clutching an even tinier dog.

"Come up, come up! I'll unlock the door!"

Hmm. For months, Lily had acted as if she had known my mother well. I hope she truly had information and wasn't just lonely for company. She looked older than I had imagined … a sliver of a woman as frail as a bird. I later found out that she had long quit driving and was somewhat of a shut-in, dependent on others. I handed her some flowers I'd picked up and resolved to make the most of this visit, information or not. It was my birthday, after all. And Lily hadn't forgotten. We had 7 PM reservations for dinner at a popular restaurant/casino combo that had a glorious reputation.

"We'll hang out and have a great time! It's a terrific way to meet new people!"

"Is there anything I can do for you before I get ready for dinner?"

"Would you be a dear and take Trixie out? That would be so helpful!"

Some fresh air did me a world of good. I changed for dinner and helped Lily into the car. It wasn't far to the restaurant, which lived up to its hype. We enjoyed a fantastic meal with impeccable service. A live pianist added to the ambiance. He played a jazzy rendition of "Happy Birthday" and the whole crowd clapped and cheered. I was delighted!

Diana with Lily Grouix.

Back at her place the days of living on adrenaline and coffee caught up with me. I thanked Lily for making my birthday so memorable as I begged out of a nightcap and made my way to bed. I slept like a baby for the next eleven hours and woke up rejuvenated. Lily was in the kitchen, and the smell of fresh coffee wafted through the air. We were having brunch on her terrace when the phone rang.

"Hi, Diana. Aaron Chapman here. I want to set a time to meet at the Penthouse tonight. Are you available?"

It was the call I'd been waiting for. I finished brunch and helped Lily tidy up. I was eager to be on my way, but not wanting to be rude, I drove Lily to the bank, the market, and her favorite store. Before I left, I gave her the scarf I'd purchased at the gallery in Port Moody.

"Oh, Diana, it's fabulous!"

I hugged her and told her how grateful I was to have spent my special day with her. I wasn't fibbing when I said it was a day I'd never forget. On my way out I strolled into Lily's memorabilia room full of articles and photos of her in her prime – including the one of her and Mom. Tears streamed down my face.

"Your mother was great, and so are you, Diana. Find the truth."

# Chapter 19
## *The Penthouse Nightclub & Bon Jovi*

I was in a great mood on my drive away from Langley. Maybe it was the feeling of accomplishment; after all I had checked some things off my long list:

1. Met Lily for the first time. (I promised myself I'd call her once a month to try to alleviate her loneliness.)

2. Made contact with Jim Millar at the Port Moody Railroad Station Museum (though nothing came of it, still, I had done it!).

3. Dinner with John Grasty gave insight about Grandmother's property AND some leads.

4. Set up tonight's meeting with Danny Filippone and Aaron Chapman at The Penthouse Nightclub!

I called my hair salon for an appointment; tonight was important.

"I need my hair to look like a rock star."

Kenji was his usual "What's up, Girl?" self. "So you want to look like a rock star, huh? Are you going to tonight's Bon Jovi concert? Rumors are the concert is canceled because his promoter didn't get the right permits."

"I don't have a ticket for tonight but I've seen him live in Tampa. He always puts on a great show." It was true: I had and he did.

Kenji gossiped on. "My friend at Roger's Arena has a friend with an extra ticket for the show tonight; he's selling it for $600 if you're interested."

I laughed out loud. "Thanks, but for that price Bon Jovi needs to take me himself. I have plans anyway, and I need a room for the night. I'm meeting Danny Filippone and Aaron Chapman and all the hotels in town are booked because of the Bon Jovi show."

"Let me see what I can do. One of my friends works front desk at the Opus Hotel." Kenji knew everybody.

"What's the location?"

"Yale town, Woman! The Opus is one of the top five hotels in the world, the regular rate is around $300 a night."

"Too pricey for my blood."

"I'll say you're a distant relative and get you a discount. Hang on a second."

By the end of my hair appointment I had a reservation at the Opus Hotel and an edgy new hairdo to boot. Kenji was good. I looked every bit the rock star.

The Opus bellman greeted me, took my luggage, and led me to the front desk. It was teeming with visitors in for the Bon Jovi gig; the sea of accents was an intoxicating hum, and I drained a glass of complimentary wine soaking it all in.

The front desk staff was friendly and helpful and my booking went through without a hitch. Inside my room I tipped the bellman, closed the door and sank into a funky orange cushy chair. My phone rang.

"Hi, Diana, Aaron Chapman here."

"Hi, Aaron." I was feeling cozy and cosmopolitan with my new do and fancy room.

"Does 9:30 at the Penthouse work for you?"

"That's fine with me."

"Remember to bring the photographs and any questions you want to ask Danny."

"Of course. See you at the club at 9:30."

I ordered dinner from room service and got ready to take advantage of the spa bathroom's amenities.

Then for no reason at all, I got nervous. And I had to talk myself down.

*You can do this. Yes, you're in a country not your own. Classy as it may be, the fact remains you're going to a strip club by yourself, and you might meet a half-brother you never knew you had. But come on. This is a part of your journey. Meeting Aaron Chapman and Danny Filippone is an important link. It's on the list. You've come from disbelief to a basement full of boxes and horse blankets to this night when some of the mystery might come together. It's another link. It's why you're here: pull yourself together. Let's do this.*

I finally felt myself relaxing as I soaked in the Jacuzzi tub, and took my time dressing. My mood shifted; I felt confident and assertive, ready for whatever the evening held.

The Penthouse Nightclub was a two-minute walk from the Opus but good sense prevailed; I drove. I circled the Penthouse in search of a spot, and that's when I spotted Danny Filippone stepping out of his white limousine, right in front of his establishment. Given what I knew of his background, I wondered if the glass was bulletproof.

The family ran the Penthouse as a "bottle club" until 1952: customers brought their liquor, and the club offered live music and entertainment. The entertainment evolved into Vegas-style chorus girls. In mafia-like drama, Joe Filippone was shot in his office at the Penthouse in 1983 during a heist.[1]

Aunt Jan said Grandfather ran the poker tables in the '50s and '60s. I parked in a small garage down the street and walked to the club. I sensed footsteps behind me. I became frightened and walked faster.

Then a man's voice said, "Hey, you come back here!"

I hurried to the Penthouse and was relieved to see Aaron waiting outside. I knew The Penthouse was notorious for being shabby and decrepit, but I wasn't expecting to be followed or harassed but I didn't mention my experience.

The layout immediately struck me as odd — you walked up the steps, turned around, climbed more stairs and out of cramped darkness double doors opened to a spacious room with a stylish bar full of beautiful, exotic women surrounded by bright lights and neon. They circled the brass poles as if hypnotized by their art while spotlights swirled all around them. Their costumes were festooned with feathers, rhinestones, and glitter … it was Vegas all over.

Aaron leaned in slightly, as if to share a confiding detail. "Saturday nights are for Cabaret Toriage, which features a bit of Vegas and New York City to spice things up. While we wait for Danny, let me tell you something about myself. I was adopted; my father died when I was four, and my mother passed away when I was twenty-two. I am of Irish descent and have carved out a life here as a local author, musician, and history buff about the city's entertainment scene."

He was easy to chat with, and I enjoyed my time with him. I turned around and saw the shimmery walls full of photographs of famous people who had visited over the years. I wondered if my mother's photo was there and then I remembered Donna's best friend, Doris Langerak, had worked here.

I turned around again, I noticed a friendly, robust man with light brown hair whose smile lit up the room. He approached me and introduced himself as Danny Filippone.

"You must be Diana. What are you drinking?"

"Scotch."

"Give her our best premier scotch and make it a double."

"Diana, may I see your mother's photos?"

I handed Danny the photo with the Roman column in the background.

"This wasn't shot in the Penthouse. Your mother was elegant, sophisticated … you look like her. In this shot, she reminds me Audrey Hepburn."

I was flattered and I thanked him shyly as I showed him

the iconic bikini photo of my mother taken in front of the bathhouse at English Bay in 1953. Danny seemed impressed – in any case, he asked for a copy of the picture. The last photo I showed him was my grandfather with my mom, taken inside the Penthouse.

Danny got quiet and looked at Aaron. All of a sudden he seemed nervous and ruffled. "I don't recognize her. Have you looked at the walls? Maybe she's there?"

Then, eager to share, he began, "Let me give you a quick rundown of the Penthouse Club's history. It was a popular celebrity hangout and an after-hours spot for visiting entertainers. Frank Sinatra, Gary Cooper, Ella Fitzgerald, Sammy Davis Jr., and Sting were among them. When Errol Flynn was in town, he was a regular. In fact, the night before he died, he was here at the Penthouse. Beyond its storied patronage, the club has been a backdrop for television episodes and over sixty-five movies."

Danny and I approached the wall, and he pointed out a few of his favorite photographs. I suggested a picture of us with the wall as the backdrop. Danny beckoned a stripper to take the picture, and all I could think was, *What am I doing in a place like this?*

The woman was stunning, with long legs and a white diva headdress adorned with giant feathers and rhinestones. When she asked if we'd like more, I smiled, thanked her and declined.

"Wait a minute! I have an employee who has been here for about forty-five years. Let's show him the photos."

Though I've forgotten the name of the man Danny introduced me to, I recall he was carrying a concealed weapon. He seemed inherently dangerous. As a bouncer, his job was to protect the girls, but his presence made me uneasy. His piercing eyes sent chills up my spine. Unfortunately, he had no recollection of my mom. I mentioned to Danny that Doris Langerak was good friends with his uncle Joe and his dad, Ross.

Danny Filippone, Diana and Aaron Chapman at The Penthouse.

I overheard Aaron say. "You should show her the private collection and secret bars. She has traveled such a long distance."

Danny shook his head no, excused himself, and went back to his office.

Aaron apologized for Danny's abrupt exit and told me he had another engagement. Before we said goodnight he gave me an autographed copy of *Liquor, Lust, and the Law: The Story of Vancouver's Legendary Penthouse Nightclub,* the book Danny had commissioned him to write in celebration of the club's sixtieth anniversary. The book was an immediate hit in British Columbia and became a number-one bestseller.

Danny reemerged seeming somewhat composed as he autographed the book Aaron gave me.

"My mother and I never discuss the club. What happens in the Penthouse stays in the Penthouse. Perhaps she knew your mom? I want to show her the photos and ask around if that's okay?"

We exchanged emails and numbers. He was shaken and muttered something bizarre about getting home, and he mumbled under his breath about his kids. I looked at him closely and thought, *Is this man my brother? He has my son's smile.* Danny gave me a big hug, and I thanked him and stopped at the powder room on the way out.

It was about a sixty-second walk to the garage. I had a distinct impression I was being watched. Again.

My heart raced. I walked faster. I was thinking about the stranger yelling at me before I entered the Penthouse when I spotted a policeman in the garage who walked me back to my car.

I locked the doors, fastened my seatbelt, and drove, never looking back. When I made it to the hotel, I looked behind me to be sure I wasn't being followed and made a beeline to the bar for a nightcap.

The bartender said, "You look like you've seen a ghost."

"Long story. I just left the Penthouse Night Club."

"I don't know who you are, but there's no way. Don't take this wrong but you remind me of a sixth-grade teacher. I can't believe you were in a strip joint. Now that's funny."

I ordered another scotch, glanced down the bar, and there sat Bon Jovi.

I laughed out loud.

# Chapter 20
## *Family Ties*

I was exhausted from last night's excursion. It'd been many a moon since I'd seen 4 AM. I needed coffee before I could begin to process the last 24 hours – or the last eight days.

I grabbed a bagel and coffee in the lobby and called Aunt Jeanne to see if it was okay if I stopped by. Twenty minutes later we were in her kitchen when Aunt Jan's name came up. Jeanne started apologizing for Jan's behavior the other day.

I was glad to talk; that scene had rattled me. "I've given that a lot of thought. I love her but that behavior was unacceptable. I want to excuse her because she's sick, but she's always been a bit dramatic about Donna. I don't know what to think."

Jeanne brooded for a moment. It seems I wasn't the only one in this family with questions, and Jeanne had quite a few. I tried to be patient with the rapid-fire quizzing that followed. At least she was taking an interest.

"Yep, Jan has always been less than straightforward when it comes to the subject of Donna. I'm still puzzled by the stories and the timeline she tells about Montreal. Was she there before or after Donna's death? Did she know Donna was pregnant?"

"Jan moved to Montreal after her divorce. Mom had a job with Mort and got Jan a job working for him, too. If Jan had gone to Montreal before my mother, she would have known Mom was pregnant. As for her whereabouts when Mom died, I've yet to solve that part."

Jeanne asked why I was so intent on finding the facts about my birth, and I told her: the sentimental side of me wanted to know the history and culture of my family; on the practical side, knowing my family's medical history made good sense: if there were health issues in the bloodline, I wanted to know.

"Perfectly reasonable. Now, how exactly did Donna meet Mort?"

"Donna worked as a hat check girl at his favorite steakhouse in Montreal. They got to know each other there."

Jeanne pondered this and asked a question I didn't expect.

"How has Vancouver treated you since your arrival?"

"The people I've met have been kind and generous. I don't feel like an outsider; I feel part of a clan."

"Tell me about your job in Florida."

"I absolutely love it. Most of our business is conducted online, but I help new associates close sales personally when needed. I also organize and lead in-store clinics and sales meetings."

Ron came in, poured himself a cup of coffee and joined the conversation.

"We grew up poor, Diana. Your grandmother had five children, and her husband – well, Dad – was a

Uncle Ron and Aunt Jeanne

gambler and a drunk. He ran off with another woman and left Mom penniless. I left when I was fourteen. I was a logger and there was work in Victoria, so I went. Your mom was just a kid – only nine years old. I really don't remember much about her."

When Jeanne brought out a photo album I took pictures of a few of them with my phone. One was young Ron the lumberjack, complete with plaid shirt. The time with them was priceless, and I relished every moment.

Jeanne knew me well enough by this time to see I needed some quiet time to contemplate all I'd learned, and when it

Uncle Ron as a young lumberjack.

was time to go she gave directions to nearby gardens.

"It's tranquil there. I go a couple of times a week to walk and meditate."

Instead, I drove past my grandmother's house on Parker Street in North Burnaby, the address on my mother's Registration of Death. Needless to say I had reasons to be curious. It was easy to locate and I took pictures from across the street. There were no signs anyone was home. A white fence surrounded the house; a massive Douglas fir ruled the front yard and pink roses surrounded the house as far as I could see. It was picture-perfect.

Feeling like an intruder and overwhelmed with the information and events of the last eight days I left Burnaby and drove to the gardens as Jeanne recommended. I needed a place to relax and reflect. Online articles described Van

Dusen Gardens as a "55-acre living museum of plants in the heart of Vancouver, considered to be one of North America's top ten public gardens."[2]

I made my way through an Elizabethan maze of hedges to a bench with a serene view and sat down to gather myself. I was deep in thought and jumped when my phone rang. It was Aunt Jeanne.

"Something just occurred to me about the picture of your mother that I need to mention. The photo with the columns in the background was taken at the Grand Opening of Casa d' Italia. It was a restaurant owned by Giuseppe Gentile and Gerry Di Salvo. Gerry's uncle is Joe Gentile. I think Joe is your father."

What? Though I'd heard the name before I didn't let on.

"Why would you think this man, Joe, is my father?"

"Your family dined at his restaurant weekly."

My jaw dropped. Joseph Gentile's signature was on the Death Registration I received and his contact information was in the paperwork; I'd sent an email but had yet to have a response. I was determined to learn more about this "Joe" Gentile and his relationship with my mother, so I left the peace of the garden and returned to the hotel business center to do more research.

All that evening my mind buzzed with Aunt Jeanne's sudden revelation. It made me think my family was somehow familiar with a relationship between my mom and this Joe Gentile man. I wondered what Jeanne – or Jan or Ron or Dot – would say or DO if they knew that I knew a Mr. Joseph Gentile had signed their sister's Death Registration.

# Chapter 21
## *Liam Cross & "The Drive"*

Liam Cross called as I was headed back to my hotel, apologizing for not reaching out earlier. An entrepreneur and Vancouver mafia history enthusiast, meeting Liam was one of the goals of this trip.

"No worries, Liam. I've been quite busy. I discovered new information about Joe Gentile."

"Interesting. Are you free tomorrow? I was thinking we could tour The Drive, maybe grab lunch in Little Italy?"

"Sounds like a plan."

"I'll pick you up at noon."

I picked up a tourist guide in the lobby of the hotel; the ad for Forbidden Vancouver Walking Tours piqued my interest. Most people confine Prohibition to American history but more than a few Canadians made their fortunes hustling bootlegged booze.

The same travel guide had a blurb about "Commercial Drive" aka "The Drive" that Liam had mentioned:

*A culturally rich and authentic neighborhood, The Drive is one of the city's best and most colorful shopping, dining and nightlight districts and is home to Vancouver's own 'Little Italy,' representing more than 60 years of Italian heritage."*

On my way to meet Liam, I thought about the tour I'd read about and the shady light it shed on the city I once perceived as squeaky-clean. I mean, I knew about organized crime in New York City and Florida, but I had no idea Vancouver had mob ties. If you were Mafia, I assumed you were Italian – you know, Gambino, Genovese, Lucchese, and Capone.

For some reason a little red flag went up about Liam Cross. I didn't understand his interest in meeting me, but I was going to take a chance and hope it wasn't a waste of time.

Then I saw the silver '59 Jaguar. Well, good afternoon, Mr. Liam Cross. Let's take a look at you.

He rolled down the window, lowered his aviators and flashed a flirtatious grin. This guy really turned on the charm. He rambled about his research, throwing crime family names and mafia facts around as we walked The Drive. I didn't hate this.

I was half-listening and taking in the scenery when he asked point-blank if I was looking for my father. I gave him my spiel … the search for the truth about my blood relatives – especially siblings – and the medical history factor. That seemed to satisfy him, so we stopped at Cafe Calabria for lunch. "Brando" greeted us with a smile and we were seated at his "favorite" table. It was clear this wasn't the first time he'd told this story.

"I was born in Calabria, Italy, and moved to Montreal when I was nine. I came to Vancouver in the '70s and opened the café in 1976. I love life, lively people, strong coffee, and passionate music."

As we settled, Liam asked to see my mom's Registration of Death. I put it and the research on Joe Gentile on the table. He glanced over it and I put it back in my briefcase.

I excused myself and told him I would be right back. I walked to the counter and asked Brando if he had a minute. Of course he did! He was Brando, the entertainer, and I was the curious tourist. I showed him the photo of my mum, and asked if he recognized her. Without hesitation, he responded, "I do."

"Are you sure?"

"Yes! You never forget a doll's face like that! She had class. Wait. This picture was taken in Montreal, not Vancouver."

As I was thanking him and about to ask more, I glanced back to give Liam a look only to catch him thumbing through my briefcase! Frustrated, I quickly thanked Brando and walked to the table to confront Liam. "WHAT are you doing?"

"Oh, nothing. I wanted another look at the Registration of Death."

"Well, YOU should had ASKED first." I was mad. I could feel my face flushing. I pounded my fist on the table.

"Enough with your games already. What are you up to? WHO ARE YOU?"

"I'm sorry. Please accept my apology for my bad manners."

He tapped his fingers on the table and started rubbing his forehead.

"I'm an independent businessman. I've lived here twenty-seven years. I've been in real estate for the last twelve but my current focus is the untold history of the Vancouver Mafia. Your relentless probing has reopened doors that have been forgotten for years."

So much for the charm; this guy was getting on my nerves. Something wasn't right. But here we were. I committed to playing this day out.

We passed a store and Liam gave his scoop. "This is the Italian Melody nightclub, run by Carlo Gallo. He worked with Joe Gentile. He got busted back in the '90s for importing heroin. He ran the Melody from prison until his death."

After a dozen restaurants and shops, we headed back. Liam suggested we try the Italian Cultural Center; maybe a historian worked there.

At the Cultural Center Liam turned to me and said, "They don't like outsiders; if you hear *Omerta*, that's Southern Italian for code of silence." Mr. Wise Guy was doing a bad job of proving his street cred. I could feel my eyebrows rise.

"I haven't done my DNA test yet, but I know I look Italian, and you look far from it. If anyone has a chance of getting her to talk, it's me."

The center housed a museum, library, and banquet room. The director was busy prepping for an event but gave me her card and asked that I try the next week.

We left the Cultural Center, and I hoped we could continue our search. Something might be off with Liam but we'd made headway – Brando recognized the picture, after all – and against my better judgment – I agreed to dinner the next evening.

He wrapped the day with what I now know was total blather ... "Life is valuable, and I'd love to spend your final night in Vancouver with you over dinner and a bottle of wine. I want to make amends for today. ... While you're still in town, I want to contact Leonardo Parisi, a journalist and an Italian historian in Vancouver. Parisi oversees the Society of Italians in Vancouver. I'll call you and let you know if I have any luck."

Whatever, Liam. I said good night, went to my room and crashed.

The next morning I packed, walked back over to the library gift shop to buy some souvenirs and went to the research room to investigate more information on my mom. The librarian interrupted my concentration.

"Mrs. Hochberg, someone else came by looking for the same magazine, same month, same year as the one you asked about."

"Was it a male or female?"

"A man. Tall, average-looking, early forties, dark sandy hair."

"Thank you." Hmph. Sounded like one Liam Cross.

He was due in my hotel lobby just after five o'clock and was a few minutes late. I hurried toward the elevator and asked Liam to wait ten minutes. But he followed me into the lift.

I raised my voice, "Why are you here? I specifically asked you to wait in the lobby."

Liam said, "I needed to make sure you were safe."

Annoyed, I slammed the door in his face. His charm had fizzled; this guy was a pain in the ass.

We walked down the street and heard music. "That's Frankie's Italian Kitchen's Sunday Jazz jam. It's always crowded."

The restaurant was bustling all right, and the food smelled divine.

Our waiter suggested the patio since it was a pleasant night. Liam ordered wine and appetizers. He professed his obsession with Joe Gentile, saying, "I worked hard investigating these men. I spent months and months researching." He whipped out his notebook filled with names of people affiliated with the mob. "You should contact James Dubro. He's a crime writer from Toronto who's written many books about organized crime in Canada. In Dubro's book, *Mob Rule: Inside the Canadian Mafia,* Joe Gentile is named the Vancouver Mafia Godfather. Joe was the Mob Boss in the 1950s and 1960s. Gentile had schemed, and Paolo Violi spearheaded it. These men set up shell companies to launder money between Vancouver and Montreal."

Liam's tales went on and on. As did his pouring wine. Did he think I didn't notice he was hoping I'd get drunk? Before dinner, he ordered a second bottle – and left the table several times, not noting I'd refilled his glass. He kept drinking, and talking and pouring and DRINKING.

He pulled out a list of the West Coast connection of Mob figures in Vancouver:

· Joe Gentile
· Gerry DiSalvo, his uncle was Joe Gentile
· Frank D'Angelo
· James Sanseverino
· Carlo Gallo
· Joe Biasi
· Frank Magasano
· Joe Romano
· Vince Luccarino
· Luigi Aquilini
· Rocco Salituro
· Gino Cicci
· Ray Ginnett
· Joe Celona

I'd had enough of this baloney. I looked Liam straight in the eye and fell just short of poking him in the chest as I let it rip:

"You are a LIAR – and a bad one at that. In the short time I've known you, I can tell WHEN you are lying. Why are you giving me the names of these dead mob men? Did you pick these up on your trip to the library?"

His jaw dropped; he was blindsided. But I was not finished with Liam Cross.

"I am a decent person, but don't screw with me. When I mentioned Danny Filippone, you changed the subject."

Mumbling and half drunk, he confessed he was sent as a spy to see what I was doing in Vancouver and what I knew so far.

"Who would tell you to spy on me?"

"Danny did. After I actually met you, everything changed.

Within twenty-four hours, I knew you were sincere – your intentions were good. I have been an ass."

Liam and I finished dinner and the two bottles of wine. He kept apologizing and begging me to give him another chance. He was clearly in no condition to drive, so we walked back around the corner to the hotel and I left him slumped in a chair in the hotel lobby. He was passed out cold within less than a minute. Let the hotel deal with him.

I went to my room. What a day! Liam Cross had turned out to be an agent from Danny Filippone sent to ply me with booze and pick my brain but I had ruined his plans. Still, I wasn't completely insulted. If Danny thought I was worth spying on then I must be getting closer to the truth. And Liam had provided a woman's name and contact info: "Charmaine" claimed to have knowledge of Joe Gentile and asked me to look her up back when I was back in Florida.

In ten days I'd made some headway.

But there was more, I knew it.

My work wasn't done.

# Chapter 22
## *Charmaine*

The trip to Vancouver was successful. I had garnered more support for my cause: Canadian family and friends were sharing more about Mom; someone would tell a story or remember something vague, and each puzzle piece made the picture grow.

And after a few fruitless back and forth emails, Liam's lady Charmaine sent a message about Joe Gentile that caught my attention.

### Subject: Regarding Joe (Giuseppe Gentile)

*Diana,*

*Joe Giuseppe Gentile helped young men from Italy by giving them wait staff jobs at his restaurant.*

*We assumed Joe had someone in his life besides family in Vancouver; he went to Montreal regularly. But he was discreet and never talked about it. We knew Joe had mob business in Montreal and Florida but that wasn't talked about … we treated Joe as the person he was with us.*

*He was five feet eight, heavy-set, and muscular. He had dark brown hair, a beautiful Roman nose, light brown eyes and light skin. He was a nice guy who took care of his friends. If he was involved with your mom, he loved her to the end. If he was just a friend, he supported her till the end.*

*I hope this gives you a bit of insight. I'm sorry I don't know more.*

*Charmaine*

# Chapter 23
## *Vancouver Life Magazine*

I emailed the Vancouver Library in search of an article from *Vancouver Life* that covered the grand opening of Casa D'Italia. I mentioned my mother was featured in the issue, included a picture taken at the restaurant and crossed my fingers as I hit send.

Adelaide, Special Collections Librarian responded with an email of the article from the 1966 edition of *Vancouver Life Magazine*: "About Town: The Social Merry-Go-Round in Vancouver and the Grand Opening of Casa D'Italia."

There was a captivating group photo of Giuseppe Gentile, Dr. Massimo Mancini (the Italian trade commissioner), and

A.R. Sacks and Betty Runcie, *Province* fashion editors. In the upper right corner was a prominent photo of Mom. The caption read, "The striking Miss Cole in a pensive moment amid the excitement of the Casa D'Italia opening night."

My mother's narrative fascinated me more and more, influencing who I had become.

Liam sent a photo of James Sanseverino, also known as Jim or Jimmy San Severino, believed to be Joe's right-hand man.

Liam sent another message: he'd obtained Leonardo Parisi's email address and asked if I would read the draft of the message he meant to send. After I made corrections the email read:

### Subject: Vancouver's 1960s Italian Community History

*Hi Leonardo,*

*I am working with a woman from the U.S. whose birth mother lived in Vancouver and Montreal for a time. Her mother died at thirty under mysterious circumstances. She was an attractive young woman who graced the social pages of Vancouver's papers and magazines.*

*Three men identified as Joe Gentile, James San Severino, and an unknown person brought this woman into Vancouver General Hospital in May 1967. The woman died at the hospital and Joe Gentile signed her Registration of Death.*

*Our goal is to uncover more about that night and her life and ask for your insights into where we might find further information about these men during the 1960s and 1970s.*

*We're prepared to share the data we've collected and are open to discussing any conditions or requirements you might have for your involvement.*

*Liam Cross and Diana Kayla Hochberg*

# Chapter 24
## *The Eighty-Seven-Year-Old Doctor*

After studying the Registration of Death, I knew the document was forged. Changes had been made to the date of birth, address, and watermark, but not the doctor's signature; it was the only part that looked legitimate.

I was excited to find Dr. C. and Marigold Hardwick listed in the North Vancouver phonebook. Butterflies fluttered as I prayed the doctor would remember my mother. A woman with a soft, cheery voice answered.

"My name is Diana Hochberg. Is Dr. Hardwick available?" To establish a connection, I mentioned the name of a friend whose dad is a philanthropist at the hospital where Dr. Hardwick had worked.

"My name is Marigold, but everybody calls me Mary. Claude has trouble hearing these days, so let me get him, and we can have a three-way conversation. Give me a few minutes to fill him in about your reasons for calling." I could hear voices in the background before Claude joined the call.

"Hello, Diana. Yes, I remember that night and I remember your mother. I knew she had a child and wondered if this call would ever come. My body may be failing, but my mind is still sharp. Maybe now I can put this memory to rest. I did what any decent human being would have done. I did whatever I could to save her."

As his voice trailed, his wife spoke up.

"My husband was a young and dedicated doctor back then. His career was just beginning, filled with goals ... and dreams of becoming lead cardiologist at the hospital. It feels like only yesterday...." Dr. Hardwick chimed in ...

"I remember that night. It was May in 1967. I had finished my rounds. I was headed out when I remembered notes I needed to add to a chart. On the way back to the nurses' station I was stopped by a colleague urgently calling my name ...

"'Dr. Hardwick, Claude!' The doctor was nervous and upset. He was as pale as a ghost and sweating profusely. I asked what was wrong. He said, 'Claude, I'm in a rush and need a favor for a new patient.' Well something like this had never happened. It was usually quiet this time of day, but of course I'd help; it's what I trained to do.

"As I walked to the room, I became convinced this request had been strange. In addition to my colleague's apparent discomfort, there was something in his tone ... I tried to tell myself that I was exhausted; I had been working long hours. I was imagining things. The patient was in a private room, which was rare back then – private rooms cost money.

"She was motionless on the bed. She was well groomed and good-looking. There was a large diamond on her engagement finger; having just purchased one for my wife, I knew it was expensive. I looked over her chart and approached the bed. She seemed to be asleep, but she flinched, and I realized she was awake and groggy. I started my examination and took notes. She was weak and running a low-grade fever. Then I heard her trying to speak, her voice but a whisper. 'Are you the doctor? I don't live here; I live in Montreal. Before I go to New York, I came home to see my parents. Where did you go to medical school?'"

"I told her I attended McGill University Medical College. She mentioned that she'd graduated from McGill with a degree in accounting. It became clear that this patient was awake, aware and intelligent. I began ordering tests and making notes in her chart. When I opened the door, there were three men. Two wore dark three-piece suits, and the third wore a pinstriped silk suit. They spoke in hushed voices and had cold, distant stares. One guy stopped me and asked, 'Is she going to live?' My body shook, and I stepped back. When I didn't respond, he pressed, 'Doc! Is she?' I went back in your mom's room and closed the door. I could hear the men's voices. They were angry.

"I wondered: did they want me to save her, or was this a convenient end to a complicated story? As I've questioned myself over the years, I realized she didn't seem to fit in with these three. I kept speculating: did the woman see something she shouldn't have? I could hear them arguing.

"The woman pointed her finger towards the door, and I walked back to her bedside. She motioned for me to lean in closer, and when I did, she whispered, 'Save me!' She was pleading. I didn't want to leave her. As I re-examined her, my voice rose so the men heard me. They were intimidating.

"I said: 'You should not die.'"

As his voice started cracking, Mary spoke up.

"He came home with his entire body shivering that night. It was as if that request flooded him with dread. When I asked him what was wrong he said he was thinking of an unusual patient situation and though I knew it remained in his thoughts and dreams, that was the last time we spoke about that night until today."

Of all the things to say after a conversation like that this sweet woman invited me to lunch the next day. Taken aback, but remembering the age on these two, I thanked her but reminded her I lived in Florida and wouldn't be in Vancouver until next summer. We said goodbye and exchanged addresses. I promised to send Dr. Hardwick pictures.

Running my fingers through my hair, I pondered that phone call and the events of the day. This breakthrough filled me with a chill. Despite seeing thousands of patients over his lengthy career, this doctor vividly remembered my mother – and three men outside her door.

But I anticipated there was more to the story. How did he know the woman had a baby? Did he overhear a conversation when the woman mentioned feeling better and planning to leave the next day for an important trip to New York for a meeting at The Plaza Hotel?

Dr. Hardwick was thirty-nine at the time of this event, and he never forgot it or forgave himself. After our conversation, I sent an email with photos of Donna as well as some of me.

### Subject: Information Regarding My Mother's Case

*Dear Dr. Hardwick,*

*Thank you and Mary for taking the time to speak with me today.*

*I have a few questions:*

*1.    Could you recall the names of the three men who brought my mother to the hospital?*

*2.    Joseph Gentile signed the Registration of Death. There is no mention of either of my grandparents on any related documents. Can you offer any insights?*

*3.    During her time in the hospital, are you aware if my mother had any visitors or company besides the three men?*

*To provide some context: I had planned to meet Mother in New York City on Mother's Day, May 14, 1967. Yet, according to the Registration of Death, she passed on May 10, 1967.*

*Any information you can provide would be immensely appreciated.*

*Warm Regards,*
*Diana Hochberg*

### Subject: Regarding Your Mother's Case

Diana,

Your call caught me off guard the other day and I've had time to reflect. It's been forty-seven years since this event. I don't recall whether she had visitors. I signed the Registration of Death Certificate with the date of death and the cause as acute myocarditis. I've signed many death certificates in all my years of practice. I have no proof this person was your mother.

All I can say for sure is that a colleague admitted a young lady to the hospital. She was placed in a private room. I was asked to do him a favor and attend to her. I did not admit her and that was the first and last time I saw her. This may not be the same person as on the Registration of Death Certificate.

I was told that she was a friend of a man reputed to be a mafia leader in Vancouver. Joseph Gentile was one of the three men. Gentile was the head of organized crime in the city at one time. His links to the mob go back over forty years with men like Joe Romano, Carlo Gallo, James San Severino, and Gerry DiSalvo.

I didn't meet any of your mom's relatives, nor did they come to the hospital. She suddenly died a day or two later; the hospital didn't have the equipment to treat her.

Dr. Claude Hardwick


### Subject: Confused

Dr. Hardwick,

I am confused; you seemed to remember everything clearly yesterday but backtracked your words today?

Diana Hochberg

### Subject: Important Detail About the Night I Left the Party

Diana,

*My wife recalls a party I left to see this patient, but thought it was before Christmas 1966.*
   *Dr. C. B. Hardwick*

I called Dr. Hardwick's home and spoke to his wife.

"Mary, this makes no sense and doesn't fit the story Claude told me the day before. Would you please ask him what compelled him to do this favor all those years ago?"

"He couldn't say no to them."

I concede that at eighty-seven years old, a man remembers many things: special moments, love lost and found, old friends, significant accomplishments, and regrets. Why would this one event weigh so heavily on his mind? He worked tirelessly throughout his career to save patients. He tried to save my mother. She was frail and terrified. What brought these three men to the hospital? Whatever it was, Donna had haunted him throughout his entire career.

I am thankful I spoke to Dr. Hardwick and his wife, Mary, back in 2015. He was a good doctor dedicated to respecting his patients. I sensed his great love for his wife and family. Perhaps he signed the Registration of Death because it was the only way for him to save her. I don't know.

Dr. Claude Edward Hardwick passed in 2017. Rest in peace, Dr. Hardwick.

And he died knowing what happened that night.

Dr. Hardwick remembered that night in May, 1967.

# Chapter 25
## *Book Lover's Paradise*

Thanksgiving in Florida means thinning crowds and less traffic; the kids have gone back to school and the tourist trade is slow. I'd been waiting for this time of year to drive down to Sarasota to explore bookshops for my research. One in particular came highly recommended, and I found it nestled in a vibrant downtown full of quaint mom-and-pop boutiques, bakeries, coffee shops, and galleries.

As I walked in I knew I was in a book lover's paradise. It wasn't busy and the owner and I chatted as I browsed and gathered books that she placed on the counter. I told her I was in the process of writing my own book – a true story about an American woman researching her heritage who discovers she was born in Canada and was sold to an American family through a black-market ring.

She said, "Wow. That sounds like a story for Billy Cox."

As it turned out, Billy Cox was a lifestyle reporter at Sarasota *Herald-Tribune* who wrote about local businesses and stories of interest. He had written a piece about the bookstore a while back that had brought a lot of traffic and sales. I wanted to talk to this guy. On the way home, I stopped by Lido Beach, set up my chair, and began making notes on a plan to tell my story to Billy Cox.

I called him the next day and was given his email address and on November 30, 2015, I sent my first message:

### Subject: My Journey: A Personal Discovery of Canada's Black Market Baby Ring

*Dear Mr. Cox,*

*For the past twenty-three years, I've been aware of my adoption. Since 1993, I have been on a journey to discover my roots. I met my biological maternal relatives in Vancouver. In Montreal I spoke with the orchestrator of my illegal adoption. Along the way progress was often hindered by bizarre events.*

*On more than one occasion I've been followed, been the victim of countless phone hang-ups, accused of being an imposter and even suspected of criminal activity in a burglary – a burglary I suspect was staged to hide the theft of ALL the research documents I'd accumulated in my investigation of my adoption and family history (other than a briefcase of notes I had forgotten in the trunk of my car).*

*But the most chilling event – one that stopped my research for years – happened in 2000, when a menacing voice on the phone threatened the safety of my son, his friends, and our family.*

*Last spring I decided it had been long enough and I resumed my quest. With the support of friends in Canada, I am peeling back the layers of the truth about my mother, Donna Koloski, and my sale to an American family through Canada's Black-Market Baby Ring.*

*Attached are a detailed account, the obstacles I've faced, and the facts I've uncovered.*

*I look forward to discussing this further.*
*Diana K. Hochberg*

I heard from Billy after the New Year.

# Chapter 26
## *8 mm Kodachrome Films*

I was wrong to assume my Canadian family understood my abandonment of them and my project. But they hadn't heard the cold-blooded threats that made me stop my research dead. But time had passed, I'd heard nothing else ... I felt safe enough to get tough and move forward.

So I converted my spare room into an office. The walls became a canvas for photos, messages, index cards, newspapers, maps of Canada – a collection of collages I named *The Donna Project.*

Aunt Jan's battle with cancer worsened and I kept sending flowers, despite her refusal to accept delivery. She wanted nothing to do with me. My obsession grew; I continued writing, trying to explain my silence.

Jeanne finally called over Christmas. She'd been through the house while Jan slept. "Remember the horse blankets and boxes you and David found when Jan had you sleep in the basement? Well, I decided it was time to investigate. Every step creaked and everything down there smelled moldy. I blew off the dust and looked through a couple of the boxes. One had twelve 8 mm Kodachrome films, each with the name 'Donna' on them. They're now safely stashed in my car." I thanked her profusely, and she promised to ship them within the week with the disclaimer:

"Understand the basement flooded at one point; the films might be ruined."

I told her I'd hope for the best, thanked her again and gave her my love. Ten days later the films arrived. As suspected, the films' age was an issue. I couldn't view them with-out a projector,

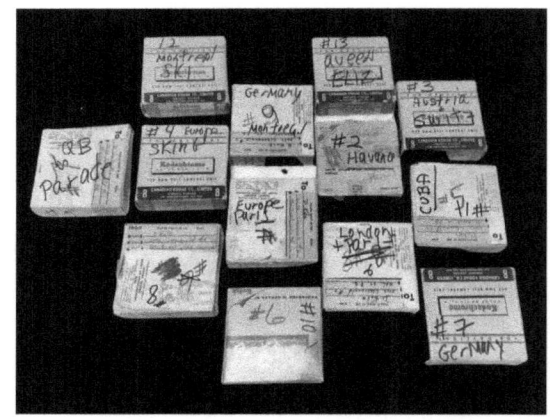

The collection of Kodachrome films.

which proved to be no small task. I finally found one online and arranged shipment.

I was on the way home from work the next day when a call came in from Uncle Ron. He was in tears. I immediately feared bad news about Jan. I pulled over. My heart sank as he shared devastating news of Aunt Jeanne's sudden passing from a heart attack. I could barely offer comfort over the weight of my own grief.

Since my last trip to Vancouver Jeanne's weekly calls had brought us closer. She had been a pillar of support for her sister-in-law during Jan's two-year battle with cancer. Last month Jeanne and Uncle Ron had marked their forty-first anniversary, a tribute to a love story that started as a blind date on December 25, 1972 and culminated in a Christmas wedding two years later.

The projector had arrived when I got home and I opened it immediately. Then some weird fear made me stop and re-seal it. I thought of Aunt Jeanne's role in getting the films from that musky basement to my home in Florida. I went to the balcony and whispered a prayer of thanks to my aunt as I watched the night sky. Summoning my courage I opened the package. There was no turning back now; I had taken the next step.

My friend Steve came over to help set the projector up. It was in excellent condition; we fashioned a makeshift screen on a door of *The Donna Project* room. True to Jeanne's warning, the films were fragile; we had to be extra careful. We took photos with our mobiles as we watched as backup. The first segment contained footage of Queen Elizabeth and the Duke of Edinburgh touring Montreal in 1959. Later my mother was skiing in the Laurentian Mountains of southern Quebec, accompanied by a woman and a little girl I believed to be Adele Wiseman and her daughter Scarlett. After watching each film, we secured it, labeled and returned it to its box.

Images of Pointe-Calumet resort outside Montreal featured an Olympic-sized pool with diving boards; Donna was diving and swimming laps. Several films featured Donna skiing in Canada, Austria, Switzerland, Paris, and Versailles. Her travels took her from Brussels to the Palais des Sports Berg Restaurant in Brama, then on to Bitburg, Germany and Kyll, Belgium.

There's a scene of Donna in Europe, pacing back and forth at a border checkpoint, her delay at the border making me wonder: 1) Why the delay? 2) Who was filming?

Here is a sample from some of the Kodachrome films Steve could salvage.

Next were films of Grandmother's home in Burnaby on Parker Street in Vancouver featuring Grandmother and her girls – Donna, Jan, and Dot. There was 1959 footage of Aunt Jan attending a graduation ceremony outside McGill University.

The last roll blew Steve and me away. After graduation Donna went to Cuba for two weeks. It was the summer of '59. She flew to Havana and checked into the Five-star Hotel Nacional de Cuba. Constructed in 1930, the architecture and style were Art Deco with elaborate chandeliers, mahogany furnishings and brass fixtures. After the Cuban Revolution, Fidel Castro made Hotel Nacional de Cuba his headquarters, declared gambling illegal, and shut down the hotel's casino.[3] In the midst of these historic events, there was Mom, casually walking outside the hotel, with the scenic seafront of the Vedado district in the background. In the next she was on the lawn next to pineapple trees and surrounded by several soldiers. They appeared engaged in friendly conversation

One of several stills from the Cuba reel used later to help identify the Cuban Revolutionaries depicted.

while the world changed around them. There were shots of a handsome man in bathing trunks – a tall, muscular figure surrounded by soldiers of the Cuban Revolution. I was shocked; **one of the soldiers looked like a young Fidel Castro!**

Steve did an incredible job cataloging the films and we took our time watching. Tears rolled down my cheeks as I watched Mom. She was so young and seemed happy, and carefree … smiling and laughing.

My perspective on life changed. There was my mother, alive and breathing, skiing, diving, traipsing all over Europe, living in high style, delayed at borders, surrounded by men in uniform, and WAS that Fidel Castro? … the questions seemed endless and it was all so exotic! I found myself longing to know her story more than ever – and wondering where I was while she trotted the globe.

As thanks for his help I took Steve to dinner at our favorite spot in Clearwater – "Flying with Jerome" – an authentic French gem I had discovered by accident. It was a pleasant evening with no talk of the Donna Project at all until we were leaving: I repeated thanks for his help and shared intentions to immerse myself in the history of Castro and Cuba. Steve's response was cool.

So I studied Cuban history, specifically Castro's rise to power in 1959. The Cuban Revolution, which culminated in the overthrow of Fulgencio Batista's regime on July 26, paved the way for the establishment of a new government under Castro.[4] In my studies I was intrigued to learn Errol Flynn frequented Cuba and was friends with Castro during this period.

Given Flynn's known visits to the Penthouse Night Club in Vancouver, a landmark in my mother's history, I felt safe to assume they might have known each other. Interestingly, two months after his last trip to Cuba, Flynn was back in

Vancouver; it is a popular rumor that he paid a visit to the Penthouse Night Club on the night he died.[5]

I found a shop that specialized in reformatting 8 mm to DVD in the historic district of downtown St. Petersburg. The next week, the shop called; the job was complete. I was delighted and excited as I went to the counter to collect my order and settle the invoice. I was greeted by the gal I'd been dealing with over the phone throughout the film transfer, a pleasant young woman named Zoe.

"Hi! I'm glad to see you. We need to speak in person. You know, the films are old and damaged; we did our best."

"Yes, I get that."

"Please complete this form? It certifies that you are the owner of these films."

"No problem."

"May I ask, how did you obtain the photos of Fidel Castro?" Unsure of how to answer her, I smiled.

"Your photos tell a story."

"Thank you, Zoe." I signed the paper, paid and started to walk away, but stopped, turned around and announced, "My mom took those."

That night on the way home, I stopped by my friend Rex's home in Tierra Verde. Rex was a Veteran. I had an idea he had ties in Washington, DC, but wasn't sure of the extent. He rarely discussed his career. Rex assumed I was there for my favorite scotch – until I quietly requested a private conversation.

Rex knew a bit about my research – it was no secret to anyone who knew me that I was on a quest for the truth about my mother. I shared the story of the Kodachrome films.

"May I see the photos? Hmm, who do you think this is here?" He was pointing to the man I thought was Castro.

"I don't know. Mom spent two weeks in Cuba and took the photos. I thought one man was Fidel Castro."

"Do you know what year your mom took these photos?"

"August 1959."

"Okay, leave me two photos, and I'll see what I can find out."

I decided not to wait for Rex. I enjoyed history and historic places so I ventured to Ybor City, Tampa. Over the years, the ethnic neighborhood had turned out several notable figures, including Mafia bosses and political activists.[6]

I parked off 7th Avenue, the streets paved with bricks and lined with swaying palm trees. A flock of red chickens and a rooster crossed in front of me. The scene was postcard-perfect.

I passed a cigar museum and was reminded of my father and his stinky Cuban cigars. Since 1900, Ybor has been famed as the world's cigar capital as well as a destination for Cuban immigrants, making it a hotbed of senior citizens well-versed in the history of their homeland.

I made my way through the streets, taking in the old world ambience. I spotted two police officers having coffee and asked if they knew any shop owners who were directly from Cuba. One suggested I visit the cigar-rolling district. I came upon a woman who appeared to be my age; she had immigrated at thirteen. She advised I come back another day since Mondays were typically quiet. I showed her one of the photos and her immediate reaction was, "What are you doing with a photograph of Fidel Castro?"

When I said the photos belonged to my mother, I could see on her face she found it odd I should have it. I thanked her and left, promising to come back another day.

Over the weekend I had friends in town from North Carolina (Dakota), and New York City (Joy) for a few days. Joy had recently been laid off; coming to Florida was a chance to regroup. I was looking forward to playing tour guide while continuing my research as we started out in Ybor City. We had lunch at Florida's oldest and largest Spanish-speaking restaurant where we savored authentic Cuban food and admired the art in every room. After a delightful meal complete with Sangria, I suggested a walk.

We meandered through the streets. It started to drizzle so we ducked onto the porch of a café and ordered coffees. I left them there on the ruse that I had an errand and went back to the cigar shop on the corner of 7th Avenue.

Señor Desi Diaz was at the front of the store.

"Buenas tardes, Señor Diaz."

"Good afternoon, señorita. Please, call me Desi."

"Desi, I was here last week."

"I remember. You are the one I told to come back any day but Monday. There is an older gentleman here today who can look at your photos." I followed Desi toward the back. He slipped behind a curtain and returned without the pictures. A man's voice spoke from behind the fabric.

"Is the man standing in the middle next to Fidel your father?"

"I don't know."

"Señorita, three of these men are part of Castro's family: Fidel, Raul, and Ramon. I don't recognize the other two men. The man wearing the bathing trunks looks large, strong, and tall. Good luck."

"Mil gracias," I whispered, as my heart beat so hard I knew it could be heard.

I walked away, absorbing these colossal confirmations from a man behind a curtain. It was hard to hold back my renewed curiosity but I did. I joined Dakota and Joy at the café and pretended to contribute to the conversation when all I could think about was the voice behind the curtain and the ever-burning question, "What was my mother doing with these men?"

When my company left, I watched the tape of Castro repeatedly. I focused on his body language, the gestures as he positioned each individual for a photograph as if in strategy.

Three weeks later I went to Rex's for dinner. When I asked if he had heard from Washington he fell silent, his expression shifted, and there was a palpable change in the atmosphere.

"I'm calling in a favor. It takes time."

Unable to stop myself I announced, "I know who's in the photos."

"The photos are not of Castro or his family."

I pressed further. "Oh, no? What gives you that impression?"

"A lifetime ago, I traveled worldwide. When you told me about the films and the places your mother visited, I felt I had to tell you that I've been to those places, too. Half the places I've been – hell, half the things I've done – are unknown to my friends. And I still have Washington ties. I need – you need – to act with care."

What or whom was he protecting me from? Was he a spy? He went on before I could ask.

"My friends in Washington want to know how I came across these images. I told them they belonged to a friend who found them amongst her mom's belongings. I was told to make them disappear."

I mentioned Ybor City to him, but I didn't reveal everything – I didn't tell him about the source that had identified Raul Castro.

But the last thing he said did nothing to discredit what the man behind the curtain said: "I can confirm one face and one name: Raul. Raul Castro. Now, will you please drop this and forget these photos? Please stop."

# Chapter 27
## *My First DNA Encounter*

Driven by curiosity about my relationship to Danny Filippone (was he my half-sibling or first cousin?), I ordered a DNA test kit from Ancestry. I wasn't sure what I was doing. Was I ready for what I might find out?

For a week the kit sat unopened on my kitchen counter. I finally spit into the tube and sent it in. Eight weeks later the results arrived. I'd no experience reading DNA tests so the information was hard to decipher. Of course I was hoping to discover family traits and pre-existing medical conditions – you know, fundamental facts. But the daunting part was bracing for the personal revelations. I took one – or three – deep breaths and decided, what the hell? Maybe if I maintained a sense of humor through this I'd have the strength to navigate the emotional rollercoaster of the mysteries of my family tree.

The ethnicity estimates were astounding:

45% Central and Eastern Europe,

21% Southern Italy & the Eastern Mediterranean,

10% Scotland,

5% Ashkenazi Jews,

5% England & Northwestern Europe,

4% Germanic Europe,

4% Ireland,

3% Cornwall,

2% The Netherlands, and

1% Nigeria.

I couldn't believe it. There had to be a mistake; these couldn't be mine.

When I finally accepted the results (remembering my sense of humor), my jigsaw puzzle of an adventure began. My aunt said my father was an Italian from Vancouver. Was she misinformed, or deliberately lying?

Ancestry messages started filling my email inbox from people asking about my family tree. I was still not sure what I was doing – until I met Cherie and Janice. Cherie was an expert connecting with people on Ancestry and Janice was a genealogist; they bombarded me with information and charts. Oddly, Janice turned out to be a maternal cousin! Both women were DNA experts and help me navigate the intricacies of Ancestry ... downloading GED matches, up-loading my DNA profile, comparing my DNA with others'– all in the interest of finding relatives.

I had reservations, but maintained a positive outlook as I worked on building a family tree and responded to those with high genetic matches. I introduced myself clearly but didn't disclose my search for biological parents. Instead, I mentioned I was new to Ancestry and that we had a match. I shared my interest in exploring family history and a willing-ness to exchange findings. To avoid making anyone uneasy, I provided only essential details. I was delighted when I received responses.

Matches came in from all over the states ... Colorado, California, Washington, Indiana, Missouri, New York, Texas, Connecticut, Virginia, and the Carolinas. With each match, the list expanded. I was disappointed there was noth-ing about Canadian relatives. This raised doubts about the

results' authenticity. Then I noticed people with exact matches consistently had the same usernames across various social
media. This made them more reliable so I incorporated those
names into my family tree.

Everything was going smoothly until someone named
Hampton accessed an email from me in which I expressed an
interest in my biological father. Over the course of seven days
in March 2016 I learned:

Hampton was Mort Shulman's nephew and had recently
begun DNA exploration, too. At some point in the process
his wife remembered Mort mentioning a photograph in a
Montreal newspaper of a cigarette girl he thought was Mom.
The newspaper had mentioned a connection between Mom
and Mort.

Hampton thought we should continue testing our DNA
to find insights into our shared family history. He had the
idea that Mort could be my father making him (Hampton)
a first cousin.

I thanked him for reaching out, affirming I wasn't surprised that Mort was involved, and told him we didn't need
more DNA testing; all we had to do was download our current results to a site for comparison.

In the end, DNA confirmed I was NOT Mort's daughter
and, boy, did I breathe a sigh of relief. I had neither considered nor desired Mort turning out to be my father. I had
never held Mort in high regard – at one point I even believed
he might have contributed to Mom's demise. I let this go and
continued my DNA adventure with a chart featuring all my
cousins. Not everyone was a willing participant. I accepted
that; a journey like this can be a slippery slope; I didn't want
to be pushy.

More and more I felt the urge to identify my biological father. I followed up on shared matches every couple of weeks.
I examined and reexamined the bits of information I had for

clues I may have missed. My distant cousin, Janice Johnston, holds a MS degree in Biology-Genetics and her assistance was instrumental. Each shared piece of our history brought us closer and enriched my understanding.

# Chapter 28
## *Billy Cox*

Not every story is exclusive, but I believed mine was. It brimmed with emotion and mystery. And I didn't just want any journalist; I wanted Billy Cox of the *Sarasota Herald-Tribune*. So our email exchange began:

### *Subject: Seeking Your Assistance and Expertise*

*Dear Billy Cox,*
*This is a follow-up on the attached email I sent a few months ago.*

*I mentioned my recent acquisition of twelve 8 mm tapes that belonged to my mother. Among them is footage filmed at the Hotel Nacional de Cuba in Havana in August 1959. In an attempt to identify people in the images I researched and found a reputable elderly Cuban gentleman in Ybor City who named three men in the photos as Fidel, Raul, and Ramon Castro. A fourth man in bathing trunks standing next to Fidel remains unidentified. He is the only one not in uniform.*

*As Mother's Day approaches, I am reminded that my mother was scheduled to meet me on Mother's Day in 1967; May 14 to be exact. She never arrived. She died May 10, 1967. I don't know the details of her death. I do know she was from Canada. I've met her family, but questions remain about her past and I hope your expertise and connections as a journalist can help.*

*Thank you for your time. I look forward to hearing from you.*
*Warm regards,*
*Diana K. Hochberg*

Billy called the next day and we arranged to meet in April. I finally had the attention of a reputable journalist in a respected publication – Billy Cox wasn't some hack that wrote tabloid blather. As our meeting approached, I tried to prepare. I didn't want to blow this opportunity. Even after several phone conversations, I didn't think he believed my story.

I made a list:

*What do you say in an interview with a journalist?*

One: Be yourself. It establishes trustworthiness.

Two: Prepare. Expect straightforward questions and be able to clarify your answers.

Three: Be enthusiastic and energetic.

I needed to let him know I'd done my research. I was fluent in Cuban history and had organized evidence that supported what I knew about Donna. I needed to tell him "my mother's story." I wanted it to resonate with and compel others. A colleague, Carlos Olivera, suggested I contact Cristina Puig, a news anchor in Tampa. If Billy Cox showed no interest, I'd see if my story caught her eye. A quick search on the Internet (is nothing private anymore?) revealed she was born in Philadelphia to Cuban parents. Perhaps this thread of camaraderie would stoke her interest.

Coincidentally, President Barack Obama's historic visit to Cuba was making news. It was the first visit by a sitting U.S. president to the island nation in nearly 90 years, as well as the first since Fidel Castro's revolution established Cuba as a Communist state.[7] The timing seemed perfect to release my mother's story.

I was taken off guard when Cristina called and bluntly asked if my grandparents and mother were part of the

Communist takeover … and if my mother was involved in the fall of the Batista government. It seemed that since I told her about my mother's photos, she assumed Mom was privy to conversations in Fidel's inner circle.

She called back Monday, expressing regret for not being able to help me. As our conversation drew to a close, she offered to reach out to a contact at the Institute for Cuban and Cuban American Studies (ICCAS) at the University of Miami for more information.

I was up early the next day organizing photos and paperwork. I picked up Steve on the way to meet Billy at the station in Sarasota. It was April 25, 2016.

At the *Sarasota Herald-Tribune* I checked in with the receptionist for my appointment with Billy. We were told to take a seat; Billy was due in twenty minutes. As soon as he saw me he said, "You looked like Donna from the moment I saw you!" – like he knew my mother personally. My instincts stirred. All he'd ever seen were photos.

We met in a conference room where folding tables were laid end to end in a rectangle. I spread my photos, notes, and documents in a timeline.

"I know you're telling the truth. I mean, look at this evidence. You've done some serious legwork here, Diana. I think we'd all like to know more about our parents, but your story is exceptional."

Steve sat close, keeping a check on me. The more Billy and I talked, the easier it was.

"Any chance I can talk to your brother, Jesse?"

"Sure, Mr. Cox, we can call my brother."

So, I called. "Hi Jesse. I'm in Sarasota at the newspaper being interviewed for a Mother's Day feature about my mother, Donna. The reporter wants to ask a few questions." There was a pause on Jesse's end before he agreed.

"Okay, I guess." I handed Billy my phone.

"Hello Jesse. This is Billy Cox from the *Sarasota Herald Tribune*. Your sister says it's okay to ask a few questions."

"Yes, go ahead."

"Did you know about your sister? How do you feel about Diana doing this?"

"I agree with her; she needs to know. She'll be able to find closure."

"Jesse, did you know you were adopted?"

I grabbed my phone as soon as I could. Jesse's voice was cracking.

"Jesse, I can't tell you how sorry I am. I'll call you back."

"Mr. Cox, let me explain. My brother's eight years older than I am; he was legally adopted in NY City. I am a Black-market baby, born and sold in Canada to a family without the formalities of legal adoption. Jesse knew nothing about this until I started my search."

Billy turned and said, "I think you have a real story here!"

Then he looked up, smiling widely, his hands spanning the air as if spinning a dream as he announced, "I see a full-page feature …we'll call it 'A Mother's Day Quest.' Diana, let's arrange another meet and photo shoot – and let's do it soon! Mother's Day is just around the corner."

We talked for several hours. His enthusiasm was convincing. I thanked him for listening and actually hearing what I said.

The ride home was quiet. When I dropped Steve off, he asked if I was okay. I assured him I was and thanked him for his continued friendship and support – especially today.

As soon as I was home I sent Billy an email thanking him for his time. I included a list of names and contact information for all my family and close friends – in case he needed to confirm anything. In a few days, I was back at the *Sarasota Herald-Tribune*. Meeting Billy Cox. Armed with my arsenal of Donna Project evidence … but I could tell instantly that something was up.

He made small talk about the newspaper business … the history of the *Sarasota Herald-Tribune* and how it was once owned by the *New York Times* … the newspaper industry is changing all the time …

This Billy was not the Billy who, only days ago, had gleefully spread his hands in the air as he relished the juiciness of the bombshell feature he had landed.

No, something about this Billy Cox was different. But he seemed to compose himself and got back to the business at hand. The more we spoke, the more I liked him. And I opened up.

"Everyone's family has secrets. I discovered my parents' years after they were gone. Despite losing them at a young age, finding out they weren't my birth parents added a bigger challenge. On my journey to locate my biological mother, I realized exploring the past can sometimes lead to undesirable outcomes. Writing this story will explain how I feel, perhaps even give me closure … after all, I was supposed to meet her on Mother's Day in 1967."

That evening I invited Rex over. I felt the need to clear the air; things had been tense between us since I'd shared the photos. I wanted to let him know that despite his warnings, positive, exciting things were coming from my discovery of the pictures. I wanted him to be happy for me.

I started out with the big news about my upcoming feature by Billy Cox.

"Rex, I have wonderful news! A reporter from the *Sarasota Herald-Tribune* is writing a Mother's Day feature story on my mother! Isn't that good news?"

His smile disappeared. He sighed and sat there with a raised eyebrow.

"What's the reporter's name?"

"Billy Cox."

"When is this going to happen? Has he seen the photos?"

"Soon. And yes, he's seen the images."

"Diana, I told you to leave this alone. You are opening Pandora's box. I covered up for you before. When I told Washington about some photos found in someone's mother's things, I didn't give a name. If this article runs, you can count on trouble. Same for those pictures. Is it worth it?"

It felt I was being interrogated. I thought of the stories he'd told of his many trips to Vancouver, British Columbia, Cuba. *Were these contrived to elicit information from me? I don't need anyone's permission to tell my story.* It was time for me to leave before I said something I'd regret.

Suddenly Billy's emails indicated he was backtracking:

### Subject: Update on Mother's Day Feature

*Hi Diana,*

*My editor has two Mother's Day items planned that I wasn't aware of – but this doesn't affect our project. We have a terrific story here; this situation actually gives us time to fine-tune it.*

*Billy Cox*

### Subject: Job Assignment Change

*Diana,*

*I am no longer writing feature stories. The decision to move me off that beat came because of my involvement in starting a union to protest driven our industry's low earnings and skyrocketing health costs.*

*I am now covering the education beat. This shift to the daily grind of routine copy was not my choice, and I'm struggling to adapt. It's a tough situation, but it reflects the current state of affairs in America.*

*Best regards,*

*Billy Cox*

A knot formed in my stomach. Something was wrong. As always, I turned to my instincts. So, I called Rex and asked point blank if he'd anything to do with the Mother's Day article not being published. He pretended to be perplexed, but to this day, I am suspicious.

# Chapter 29
## *Black Market Babies*

Researching Montreal's black-market for Jewish babies left me stunned. In the 1930s Jewish couples willing to adopt non-Jewish babies were stymied by requirements that Jewish children be placed with Jewish families. Catholics and Protestants had a supply of babies to choose from; Jewish families had none.

The Jewish community in New York amounted to three million people after World War II and included thousands of childless couples desperate for infants – but almost all the Jewish children available were older, their parents dead, their families disintegrated. This situation fed the Montreal baby ring.

I looked into every media outlet available; all reached the same conclusion: human trafficking was alive and thriving, and illegal adoptions were an ongoing practice in both the US and other countries. It became my hot button: I couldn't stop reading about Black Market Babies.

In February 1954, newspapers across North America announced the results of an American and Canadian police joint investigation of "Black Market Babies," exposing a ten-year operation in Montreal in which infants of unwed Catholic, French-Canadian mothers were being sold to desperate Jewish couples in New York. The price per child ranged from $2,500-$10,000; the business was a $3-$5 million dollar operation.[8]

A series of independent rings in Montreal had a system in place that included maternity boarding houses where the children were born and depots where the infants were housed while the business of baby peddling was settled.

It was horrifying. Spotters trolled the city for pregnant women who seemed needy. Potential adoptive parents heard about baby rings through the grapevine. Scumbag salesmen worked New York City apartment blocks. Shady lawyers helped parents secure false birth documentation to obtain Canadian passports and U.S. visas for the children. Pregnant women were sent to U.S. cities to give birth, newborns were smuggled across the border by couriers with connections to organized crime – the black market for babies boomed: between 1930 and 1975, several thousand Canadian-born children were adopted by families in the United States. Most were white infants, the children of unwed mothers.[9]

The next series of articles blew me away. It claimed Catholic psychiatric hospitals exposed orphans to experiments with electric shock, chlorpromazine, LSD, chemical sterilization, and lobotomies. Infants waiting to be adopted were kept in DuPlessis Orphanages all across Canada, as the article "Black Market Baby Ring, From Canadian Orphanages, Catholic Nuns, to Jewish Families" detailed:

*The Jewish community of three-million in New York after World War II included thousands of childless couples desperate to adopt babies. However, virtually the only Jewish children available were older children whose parents had died or whose families had disintegrated.*

*Jewish couples willing to adopt non-Jewish babies were stymied by adoption and child placement legal provisions requiring children to be placed in adoptive families professing the same faith as their own. The result was that Catholics and Protestants had a supply of babies to choose from, while Jewish families had none.*

*This situation helped feed the international baby ring that operated in Montreal from the 1930s to the 1950s. Thousands of French-Canadian babies were supplied to Jewish couples – primarily in New York, but also in Florida, Los Angeles, Detroit, Cleveland, Chicago, and throughout Canada. A U.S. Children's Bureau report in 1955 stated, "Of all the black-market cases that have come to light, the great majority are known to have involved Jewish couples."*

*Louise Wise services, New York's only Jewish adoption agency, told him and his wife those applications outnumbered babies twenty to one. Many Jewish couples didn't even bother applying because they knew it was hopeless...*[10]

It was chilling to know I was a product of this era. I mulled conversations with Mort Shulman. I was sure he took care of all the nitty-gritty details for my mother, claiming to be a family friend doing a good deed. In reality he was an unscrupulous businessman in the business of peddling babies – human trafficking at its lowest form.

Liars always have trouble keeping up what's true and what's not. That's the only explanation I had for him blurting out his comment about my 'birth mother,' dispelling a lifetime of family history, as I knew it. He started my beleaguered journey to unravel details of my existence. My mother wasn't Jewish, but her baby ended up in New York City with an Orthodox Jewish family. I was one of thousands.

Dr. Karen Balcom, a noted expert on this topic, introduced me to Harold Rosenberg in 2016. They knew the process of baby transport from Canada to the States without legal paperwork. Harold was a black market baby himself: sold in 1949, he found out about his adoption when he was thirty-five and was still searching for his roots. His adoptive father paid $1800 for him. Over the years, he hit many a brick wall and followed false leads ... sound familiar? Like me, he had no official records of his adoption, and the birth record kept by the synagogue was a fake.

When he asked how I'd come to my journey, I told him about Mort being a well-known businessman who had arranged everything, and how I discovered this was not his first time.

"Twenty-one days after my birth, he took me across the border to Plattsburgh, NY, then Lake Placid where he sold me to the Hochberg family with no documentation. The zinger was that Mort's father, Jay Preston,

Harold Rosenberg

was a business colleague and friend of my adoptive father, Manny Hochberg."

As talk turned to Donna's gap-filled lifeline, I asked if he knew how someone's identity could be erased, adding that I'd considered the Witness Protection Program as a possibility. At the time it seemed like a wild card, but nothing surprised me anymore.

The next time we spoke, Harold had done some digging – confirming some things I knew already … like Donna's work as a bookkeeper for H.M. Shulman & Associates and her apartment at the Clanranaid complex … and some I didn't.

Donna's apartment was across the street from Congregation Shiloh, a small synagogue managed by Rabbi Hershom. Harold attended services there with his dad and played outside during holiday breaks. He remembered seeing a woman walking a Havanese – the national dog of Cuba – across the street.

I was certain the woman he saw was my mother, Donna.

# Chapter 30
## *Landing on the West Coast*

I was in Walnut Creek, California, for a wedding and research meetings. I spent quality time with family before getting down to business.

A friend, James Hourston, had solid family connections with Vancouver General Hospital and had offered to look into Mom's missing records on my behalf. Despite his prominence, Medical Affairs department's response to his queries led nowhere:

*"We are unable to assist you in searching for information regarding Diana Hochberg's mother's passing."*

Determined to help, James reached out to acquaintances that may have known my mother, including Danny Filippone.

Another friend, Rick McCartie, helped me research local churches.

While in Walnut Creek, I received several detailed emails I was hoping could shed some light on the adoption/legal situation and my Canadian citizenship.

### *Subject: Mafia Ties and Secret Adoptions: A Cross-Border Saga*

*Diana,*
*I have a natural inclination to assist those unfamiliar with the legal system.*

*Have you come across the names Glazer or Buller? They were involved in undercover adoptions, aiding in the transfer of children from Montreal to families in New York.*

*Joseph Gentile lives in Vancouver and has ties to the New York Mafia, including the Bonanno, Gambino, and Gotti families. Joey "Bananas" Bonanno has since retired to Arizona. Notably, the FBI, after a decade-long investigation, incarcerated John Gotti, also dubbed the Teflon Don, alongside Joe Gentile, Frank D'Angelo, and Jimmy Sanseverino.*

*Joe Gentile and Gerald D'Salvo co-owned Casa D'Italia. D'Salvo's son has been seeking information about his father. Another report claims Joe was the Mafia boss, with allegations linking his brother's restaurant to the operation.*

*John Papalia visited Montreal to meet with Viola and Cotroni for three days. The meeting, led by Viola and Joseph Gentile, aimed to establish shell companies for laundering money.*

*Joe Gentile and Paolo Violi share numerous connections. Joseph is mentioned in several publications, including Iced: The Story of Organized Crime in Canada. The book, along with James Dubro's Mob Rule: Inside the Canadian Mafia, references Joe several times.*

*Stella*

### Subject: Gratitude for your insight/James Dubro

*Dear Stella,*

*I greatly appreciate your assistance. You are the second person to mention James Dubro.*

*I have some experience with the American legal system but without a sworn statement from Mort Shulman or a relative, I can't verify my Canadian birth.*

*Thank you again for your help.*

*Best regards, Diana*

My father was fascinated with the Mafia and immersed himself in books and articles, so I grew up hearing about these subjects more than most. Whenever a new Mafia movie came out, I couldn't help but chuckle; the plots were just the tip of the Mafia iceberg as Manny Hochberg told it.

When I searched the Internet for Giuseppe Gentile, I found his obituary. He died January 28, 1995. This eliminated him as the *killer's voice.*

While I was boarding my flight to Vancouver, James Hourston called to check my ETA. Once on board I was delighted to hear I'd been upgraded to first class. I wondered if James had anything to do with that pleasant surprise.

In Vancouver, everything went smoothly, and I proceeded to the luggage carousel. As I stepped out of the airport, I looked toward the right corner and saw Rick McCartie holding a *Welcome, Bienvenue* sign. It was the first time we'd met in person, but we'd texted and talked so much that I felt like I'd known him for years. On the way to the hotel, we reminisced about the last thirteen months.

We met in a group on a Vancouver Facebook page where members share photos of the "City of Light" and tell stories of the past. Rick had been investigating anything he could about Donna. He held a similar devotion and dedication to his mother, Althea, and was eager to help.

As I was settling into my room there was a knock on my door; it was James Hourston.

"Hi there! I'm making sure you arrived safely and are pleased with your room."

"I am! This view is spectacular!" (Did I mention my room had been upgraded, too?)

"Tomorrow is going to be a long day, Diana; rest up, I'll see you in the morning."

"Thank you for suggesting this hotel and dropping by. Goodnight. I'll see you soon!"

*Good morning, Tuesday.* Parting the curtains I was greeted by a magical view of the city. I pinched myself to be sure I wasn't dreaming. James and I had an 11 AM appointment with his father's lawyer and he showed up with coffee for two.

Collin, the Hourston family's attorney of twenty years, had expertise in immigration, family law, real estate, criminal law, and child custody. After spending a little over an hour in his office, the discussion turned into disappointment. The crux of the matter, as outlined by Collin, was the absence of any wills from my mother, grandmother, or uncle – without them I had no rights.

Overwhelmed by a mixture of discouragement, disillusionment, and stress, I began to cry. This wasn't about a will or money; I was here trying to claim my Canadian birthright.

"I believe you," Collin said, handing me his business card. "I'm riding my motorcycle to Denver for ten days. Have you ever been to Denver?"

I told him I was there in 2001 for work and was planning a long weekend at the end of October.

James and I left the building, feeling dismayed. As we headed towards Chinatown I tried to lighten the mood. "Let's make the most of the day."

We wandered through Gastown and made a short stop at the Vancouver Police Centennial Museum, searching for clues about the local mob. After coffee we headed back to the hotel. James left me to rest and freshen up for dinner at his place.

James's place in the West End was built in 1927, and I felt transported to the Gilded Age. His backyard terrace had a lovely table set for three. What a wonderful surprise! Rick was joining us! We discussed plans for the week in Vancouver, and I warned them it would be hectic. Both were worried about me walking the streets of the city alone; it seemed I had picked up two bodyguards – and that was fine by me.

At the end of the evening I thanked James for a fantastic time, and Rick drove me back to the hotel. He wanted to come up for a few minutes to discuss tomorrow's plans. He said he knew of a lovely breakfast spot, and afterwards we could head

Rick McCartie, Diana, and James Hourston

over to the First United Church.

I had contacted the church beforehand, and told the church manager a little of my saga … and that my grandparents were married there on March 22, 1929. She was delighted with my story and told me about Reverend Bob Burrows, who had been with the church four decades. The next day, I received an email:

### Subject: Re: Grandparents and the church

*Dear Diana Hochberg,*
*I look forward to meeting you, and have a book I think may interest you. I am forwarding your email to some folks who might know of the event or have information on historical records.*
*Rev. Bob Burrows*
*First United Church Community Ministry Society*

Rick joined me at the church where Rev. Burrows greeted us and gave a tour lingering for a bit in the room where my grandparents were married.

He gave me a copy of his newest book, *Hope Lives Here,* saying, "This book is for you because your grandparents were married here during the Great Depression. I mentioned them in these pages."

We discussed my quest and talked about my aunts' refusal to see me. Rev. Bob reassured me, "When the time comes, you'll get the answers." The reverend's work and dedication to the community moved me. We said our goodbyes, and I turned to look at Rev. Bob … until the next time.

Diana and Rev. Bob Burrows, photo by Rick McCartie

We left to meet James at a coffee shop off East Cordova. I had ulterior motives for my choice; I believed the owner's father might have been Joe Gentile's son. I asked the barista if I could speak with the owner. By this time James was there. A man came out from the back room, introduced himself as Wayne and asked if everything was okay. Satisfied that it was, he seemed irritated to have been summoned from his kitchen duties and asked how he could help. My knees began to tremble, and my voice became stiff, but I summoned my reserve and got to the point.

"I'm on holiday from the States, visiting relatives and friends in Vancouver."

I ignored James' step on my foot under the table.

"I believe your father knew my mother, Donna Kolosky? She and my family used to eat at his restaurant in the '60s. Would you take a look at one piece of paper?"

"Okay." He appeared nervous for a split second when I handed him a copy of my mother's death registration, then took one look at the photo and said,

"In 1967, I was fifteen. I know nothing; please leave." He turned abruptly and went back to his kitchen. Rick and James could sense my distress. I knew it was a gamble coming here. We left our lattes unfinished and left as asked.

I guess my bluntness had addled my 'bodyguards.' James decided Chinese food would make us all feel better. So we headed out to the Pink Pearl for dim sum.

They both tried to make me laugh, trying to help me forget Wayne's reaction. But could you blame him? Once, his father was considered the godfather of Vancouver; I'm sure he was used to questions now and then.

After lunch, I told the guys I needed to catch the SeaBus to North Vancouver. I had a Happy Hour date with my friend Francine. James had to be elsewhere and I told Rick I was taking this adventure alone. I assured him I would be fine. He insisted I text when I got to North Vancouver.

"I am not comfortable with you meeting a stranger."

"That's sweet, but only a few days ago, you were a stranger. I'll be fine."

Waterfront Station was crowded wall-to-wall, reminiscent of Grand Central. I looked for signs for North Vancouver; if I hurried I could still catch the next SeaBus. I was breathless by the time I arrived at the waiting area.

The trip took fifteen minutes and true to my word, I sent an "I'm here" text to Rick. His quick response carried a note of caution – basically that I was in uncharted territory and needed to watch my back.

I recognized Francine right away. We had agreed to wear hats. Hers was a stylish caramel-colored Fedora with a black band; mine a practical packable navy canvas from L.L. Bean.

We walked along the pier, with Francine pointing out landmarks … Lonsdale Quay, known for its stunning views of downtown Vancouver and bustling with local artist galleries, shipyards, restaurants, and shops. At Pier 7 Restaurant and Bar, we sat at a table on the waterfront; Ted Turner's yacht was in view. Francine mentioned they were friends, prompting me to jokingly suggest she should have invited him to join us. Happy Hour was in full swing and we ordered chocolate martinis. I had a lot of questions.

"How did you and your family end up in Vancouver?"

"After I graduated from Weston College of Business, I landed a job at a boutique brokerage firm. There were ten major principles – and this gets interesting, so pay attention. They underwrote a compromise with Afton Mines, a copper mine in British Columbia. The stock started at eleven cents and swiftly rose to seventeen dollars and fifty cents. It kept splitting and splitting, eventually becoming a vast fortune." She was whispering as if the walls had ears.

I knew enough about finances to figure that this was either an outrageously good deal or insider trading. Francine went on.

"I watched as six men became multi-millionaires in six weeks. And they all met regularly at Casa D'Italia on Hornby Street. I didn't know it then, but that was where the money laundering was going on. I was young, and the older guys hit on me constantly. Jimmy Hoffa, and other players of the day were patrons before his disappearance."

The subject turned from our careers to my quest for my mother.

Out of thin air, Francine said, "They know you're here."
*What was she talking about?*

"They're watching us and know where you're staying."

I excused myself for a few moments to mull this weird conversation over, debating whether or not to call Rick.

I didn't. I went back to our table, and ordered an appetizer and another drink and was grateful when the conversation moved to health issues and our children when Francine uttered another out-of-the-blue blast:

"Your parents are dead."

"How do YOU know?"

"I see events."

"Are you hallucinating? What ARE you talking about?"

"I've had remarkable senses since I was a child, including clairaudience, clairvoyance, clairsentience, and claircognizance," Francine explained.

I was literally at a loss for words but – having visited psychics and mediums I recognized some of the lingo – SOME of it.

We took some pictures and, at Francine's insistence, headed over to St. Paul's, a Roman Catholic Church founded in 1884. I never asked why.

I needed to catch the SeaBus back, so I thanked Francine and we said goodbye.

All she said was, "I hope we see each other before you leave town."

I told her I'd try as I headed off. Aboard the SeaBus, I sent a text to Rick letting him know I was on my way. At this point I felt like someone needed to know where I was. Good grief, what a Happy Hour that had turned out to be.

Back in the lobby I shared the details with Rick.

"Let me to go to your room with you. I'm worried about you being alone tonight and I have something important to tell you."

What now? I couldn't imagine anything to top the odd time I'd had with Francine.

"There's a chance my father and Donna knew one another. Like her, he was an avid swimmer and they often used the same pools. I should have told you sooner."

We both jumped as the phone rang and jangled the silence, my "hello … hello?" meeting dead air.

I left the room for a few minutes to gather my thoughts and returned to find Rick passed out on the sofa. I left him there. It had been a long day for both of us and – to be honest – after Francine's odd behavior it was a comfort not to be alone – at least he wasn't whipping out a crystal ball.

I jumped again as the phone rang – again. This time it was my paternal cousin Gabriel confirming dinner at his house this Friday at 6 PM, which was delightfully normal.

"I have a call in to my daughter and her husband to see if they can join. You're welcome to bring a guest."

"Thank you! I'm going to ask my friend, James."

# Chapter 31
## *New Westminster*

The knock at the hotel door urged me out of bed. Through the peephole no one could be seen. Then I saw the note on the door:

"I ordered room service ~ Up and at 'em. ~ R"

There was a pink rose on the tray with breakfast. As I ate I jotted notes from yesterday. Another message read, "Meet you outside hotel at 9 AM ... on to New Westminster Archives."

I looked into New Westminster Archives a year ago. The archivist connected me with Barry Dykes. From the beginning, Barry made my search seem important. The distance between us and the fact that we'd never met didn't stop him from making me feel I was there as he dug through high school yearbooks ... when he discovered two photos of my aunts – both Jan and Dot – at Trapp Tech. Doris Langerak, was listed, too. She'd graduated ahead of Aunt Jan. In class pictures from '49, Janet Koloski was standing in the back row, second from the left. But no Donna.

I contacted all schools in and around the vicinity but found no records of my mother. This didn't match Aunt Jan's claim that all her girl siblings attended school. My mom, the only one to go to college, had no records. It was weird. I wasn't sure about Tom's (aka Freddie's) education, but knew

Ron attended until he was fourteen, and I knew Uncle Tom/ Freddie was fluent in multiple languages and had left Canada when he was twenty-six.

Barry was the first person who hadn't been frightened away or let me down when he learned the details of my search. In fact, he went over and above – supplying the addresses of my aunts and uncles, a list of local churches, and my grandmother's residences from 1937 to 1955. The first, *The Royal Apartments*, was home to my family for two years. Another apartment building, now gone, was captured in a photograph alongside *Arlington Apartments* and painted by famous Vancouver artist Joe Plaskett. The painting was so vivid that I could almost hear creaking stairs and howling winds.

I couldn't wait to meet Barry Dykes.

At the archives, Barry's coworker greeted us with a broad smile and a cheery hello and introduced the tall handsome man who strode behind him ... "this, my friends, is Barry Dykes."

Barry and I exchanged greetings as if we were old friends and I offered to treat him to lunch – he had done so much for me, I wanted to show my appreciation.

"Any other time I'd love to, Diana, but today I'm behind schedule and a bit shorthanded. Maybe next time."

Barry Dykes and Diana

"I understand," I said. I handed Barry *Hidden History of St. Petersburg* by Will Michaels and explained, "Michaels is St. Petersburg's resident historian. Considering your work, I thought you'd enjoy this. It was released in July."

"Oh, Diana, how wonderful! Thank you."

"Barry, I can't express how much I appreciate your time and effort in researching my family's history."

"What are your plans after you leave here?"

"I'm gathering information from various sources, following up on leads … I'm writing a book to release my story to the universe. I'd like to include you."

"I'm flattered! Do save an autographed copy for me! You might find a visit to New Westminster Library helpful. There's a painting by Joseph Francis Plaskett on display there that you shouldn't miss."

Rick and I exchanged glances, declaring in unison, "Next stop."

Observing Barry at work with his team was enlightening; photos and negatives were digitized and stored in an online database creating a valuable source for Vancouver history buffs. They were a busy bunch, so we took some pictures and took our leave, thanking him again and again for his diligence and assistance.

Next stop, of course, was New Westminster Archives. It was raining monsoon-like so Rick dropped me close to the door and I went inside. While I waited I studied a brochure of the library's history. Established in 1865 … British Columbia's first library … houses an impressive collection of genealogical and local history resources.[11] I was in Heaven. To think my grandmother and her children lived in this area during the Great Depression. As I wondered if they'd stood right where I was, the sense of what I was doing – my research, the Donna Project – seemed larger than ever. My ancestors' home was the subject of a famous painter's work! We were literally a part of history!

Not long ago my uncle and aunt shared that my grandmother met Joe Plaskett while waiting tables at the Aristocrat

Restaurant. An online search showed his works are displayed in public art galleries across Canada, from Prince Edward Island to Vancouver Island; notably, he is honored at the Massey Theatre in New Westminster! In my excitement I hadn't understood that Barry was telling me Joseph Plaskett's paintings were on exhibit at the New Westminster Library NOW. I couldn't believe the luck of my timing. I was elated!

The librarian offered to check her files to see if there were records of my family member's library cards while we were visiting the exhibit and asked me to stop on the way out.

Meanwhile, Rick and I spent an hour admiring Plaskett's artwork, with a special focus on the *Arlington Apartments* painting. My grandmother and her children lived there for two years, a fact that brought tears to my eyes.

Diana with Joseph Plaskett's *Arlington Apartments* in the New Westminster Library Plaskett Room. Photo by Rick McCartie.

"Your grandmother lived here with her kids," Rick said, his voice breaking with emotion. We cried together as we absorbed the art – the depth of emotion in Plaskett's work. I wanted to own it, but the price was far beyond my budget. The profound connection between his art and my Vancouver family was priceless.

On the way out I checked with the librarian; she'd found a card with the initials "C. Koloski." I left my contact information with her in case she came across more.

Rick had an errand across town and dropped me off at a hair appointment James had booked for me. It was close to my hotel and it was a beautiful afternoon, so I was walking back to my building when I knew I was being watched. I took a detour and went around the block on a different path. As I passed the corner store, I saw a reflection. I couldn't tell if it was a man or a woman so I ducked under a storefront awning and started taking pictures.

A man came out of the shop. "Do you need help?"

"No." I fibbed and said I was admiring his window displays when in fact I was hoping for a photo of the person following me. I thought I made it back to the hotel safely until I entered the elevator and a stranger followed. I purposefully pressed the wrong floor button, dialed James's number and told him what was going on.

He arrived within minutes. "Diana, don't you want to report this to the police?"

"No. I don't have time for such nonsense. I need to dress for dinner."

Our reservations at Giardino's Restaurant were for 8 PM. We were early and had a cocktail at the bar before being seated. James knew everyone and remembered every name. I met Chef Massimo, who was kind enough to spend a few minutes with us; in the course of conversation I asked if he had known my mother.

"Do you have a picture?"

I showed him the photo of Donna inside Casa D'Italia.

I could tell by his expression that he recognized her but he denied it:

"No, I never met this woman. I wouldn't forget a face like that."

I thanked him, gave him my calling card and said, "Let me know if your memory returns."

I told James he really knew how to make an impression on a woman.

"It's too bad you're gay."

He smirked and said, "We'll talk about that in the morning."

# Chapter 32
## *Day At Legacy/Evening At Gabriel's*

**James and Rod Hourston**

The phone rang. "Good morning! James here, reminding you of our 11 o'clock at Dad's place." I squinted at the clock; it was 7 AM.

"Why on earth are you up?"

"Dear, I haven't been to bed," he said, chuckling. "I'll see you in a few hours."

Against my body's wishes I emerged from the covers.

James was prompt and very polished for someone who'd been up all night. He looked like a model off a magazine cover. Cobalt blue slacks, a nude long-sleeved shirt, Oxford shoes, designer belt ... and of course, a matching umbrella. Not to be outdone, I changed into black designer slacks, a silk blouse, and gold jewelry.

"Listen," James almost whispered, "I need a favor from you."

"Name it."

"My father would disapprove of my lifestyle, and I rarely bring anyone with me, especially a woman. If he likes you, he'll approve everything I do, which is important to our quest; he has connections at Vancouver General. So ... you know."

I said, "Oh, I know. You want me to act like a girlfriend – isn't that what 'girlfriends' do?" I gave him a sassy wink.

161

Legacy Senior Center was a 'boutique senior residence' (James's words) – more like a deluxe retreat if you asked me: six stories of luxurious suites with premium amenities and five-star concierge services for every want or need an active (older was never mentioned) adult might have.

James introduced me to his father as a friend on holiday researching my family history. He left us to get to know each other and immediately began canvassing the dining room with my mom's picture. I thought it was a little forward, but, hey, I was just a girlfriend.

"So, Mr. Hourston ..."

"Just call me Rod. That's what my friends call me."

"Okay. Rod, tell me about yourself."

"Well, I was born in Vancouver in 1922, the second of four brothers. After high school, I went to University of BC in 1941 then left to serve in WWII. I was a bomber pilot." He grinned at me. "The dames loved me."

"When the war ended, I went back to school ... graduated with a master's in zoology. In '47, I married the love of my life, Evelyn Johnstone. Sixty-seven wonderful years we had ... I lost her in 2014.

"I was a biologist in Ottawa for two years then came back to the West Coast with my family. I retired in 1980. I was on the Board of Governors of the Vancouver Public Aquarium for years ... proudly left that post with the title of Honorary Life Governor."

"Wow, Rod! That's quite a life. Thanks for sharing."

I showed him the bikini shot of my mother at the Casa D'Italia photo.

"Mamma Mia! She was stunning."

"Do you recognize her?"

"I'm sorry to say I don't."

When James was back he told Rod how our meeting with Collin wasn't the success he had hoped for. Rod perked up.

"Well, tell him to use all my contacts, Son! There must be folks out there who knew this beauty. Put anything your girl needs on my bill."

"Thank you, Rod! That is so kind."

"What age would she be now?"

"Seventy-nine next month ... seventy-nine years old, Rod."

He turned to his son and said, "She's a keeper," James agreed.

I left them a bit to mingle and show photos of Mom and Grandmother but no one seemed to remember them.

Rod stood and asked, "I need to go to my rooms for a moment. Before you leave, would you care to see my apartment?"

"Well, of course we would!"

James whispered, "Wow. He never asks anyone to do this."

"Your dad is amazing," I whispered back.

His suite was in the corner with a great view of the city. The décor was classy in an understated way. The only component missing was the star of his show, the love of his life, Evelyn.

As I hugged him, I noticed his Air Force hat. "Rod, may I?"

"Of course," he said.

So, I put the hat on and took a selfie. He smiled. "That hat never looked so good. That photo will be famous one day."

I thanked him for everything and we said good evening. James said, "My dad fancied you."

"I was just myself; your dad is great!"

## Gabriel and Sylvia

I had dinner plans at my cousin Gabriel's home. It was our first meeting. I picked up a dessert and a bottle of wine. I heard Gabriel was a "kick-ass horn player" and in high demand on the city's lively jazz circuit.

Gabe and his lovely wife, Sylvia, greeted us warmly. I had wine on the deck with Gabriel, while James and Sylvia talked indoors. As I took in panoramic views of the city, Gabe started asking questions; for the first few moments I felt like I was being grilled.

I shared my mission to learn my family's history and told him of another possible relative I'd been in touch with, James Van Velson. "He claims you two are first cousins, referring to it as the 'Route intrigue.' I've seen the Route name on the Family History Tree on Ancestry."

Sylvia was a fantastic cook and had gone all out. We ate, drank, ate, and were very merry. When I showed Mom's photos. Gabe was overcome with excitement, and vowed to order a DNA kit ASAP. As we said goodbye, he invited us to his performance the next night.

"Bring your boyfriend."

"James is nice, but I'm not his type."

"Are you sure?"

"Very sure. Everyone who meets James falls in love."

"Bring him anyway – and anyone else you want."

On the drive to my hotel, the conversation drifted to family – and family secrets – and James dropped an unexpected bombshell:

"While we're discussing little known family facts ... I have a son."

This trip was turning out to be A TRIP.

# Chapter 33
## *A Whirlwind Visit*

Barry Peacock met me in the lobby just as the elevator door opened.

"Good morning! I hope you wore your walking shoes."

We headed to breakfast at the Sylvia Hotel in the West End, chosen, according to Barry, because it "seemed like a place Donna would have liked." Coincidentally, it wasn't far from the bathhouse of the bikini photo shoot.

He knew most of my story – the adoption, my Canadian roots – all the basics. We discussed the mystery of Donna's death and Vancouver Hospital's involvement. After breakfast headed to the bathhouse, snapping pictures in the same spot Mom had posed. I was thrilled when he insisted on helping me investigate connections in Montreal and Vancouver.

### Anastasia

At the United Ukrainian Hall of Canada, a woman asked if she could help and I told her I'd recently discovered family roots in Ukraine, and that I was looking for people who might have known my relatives. I heard singing from inside and Anastasia explained, "The young people, they are keeping tradition alive. You should come back when the seniors are present; surely some of them knew your relatives. They are part of the congregation who built this structure in 1928." She guided me into a room where young people in traditional Ukrainian dress danced and sang.

Before leaving Florida, I contacted Forest Lawn Funeral Home and Memorial Park. I had visited the cemetery before – on my first trip to Vancouver in 1994 – but now, armed with more information, I felt I had the documentation needed to justify more inquiry. Apparently my questions were beyond a phone call; I needed to visit in person. So, here I was with Donna's Registration of Death in hand, ready to learn something new. Somewhere in another office I could hear a man speaking with a heavy German accent; it had to be Hans – the man I had traveled 3,000 miles to see.

"Ah, Mrs. Hochberg, we meet at last. I'm currently with a bereaved family, and my day is full – but my associate Andrew Chen can help you. If you'd please excuse me, I'll let him know you're here."

A few minutes later, someone was behind me. "Good afternoon, Mrs. Hochberg. I am Mr. Chen."

"Good afternoon. Please, call me Diana."

"Of course. My office is right this way. What brings you in today?"

"I have reason to believe my mother, Donna Koloski, is buried here – as are other family members." I presented the documentation of Donna's death.

After a few minutes he sat across from me, clutching the file I longed to see. I told him I wanted to thank the man in charge of my mother's funeral and burial arrangements.

"I'm afraid I'm not at liberty to provide that information."

"Mr. Chen, it's my mother."

I placed Donna's Registration of Death in front of him, looked him in the eyes, and pointed to the responsible party's name: Joseph Gentile. The room was silent.

"According to the files you don't owe any money; everything is taken care of. This includes perpetual care."

I kept my eyes on his as I said, "The name on the document is Joe Gentile."

"I'll be right back." He left the room and the paperwork open on his desk. I was in the process of going to his side and taking photos with my phone when he reappeared.

I was surprised when he handed me a big sheet of paper.

"Here's a map to the graves you seek."

No kidding? Wow. If this was for real, it was a break-through I hadn't expected.

"Thank you so very much, Mr. Chen. I'll go now while there's still daylight."

I went to Grandmother's first, flowers in hand. I was mor-tified Jan had dishonored her mother by burying her at the bottom of a hill. Grandfather and his second wife were bur-ied on higher ground; her sister and her husband were buried not far from them. It was grandmother all alone at the bot-tom of the hill while the rest of them looked down on her.

Donna's was the last grave I visited; it was high up the hill, near a tree, with a lovely view of Vancouver's waterfront. I wondered what everyone was thinking when they buried my mother; she was so young and seemed so vibrant. I sat beside the grave and placed a pink rose on her headstone.

I thought cemeteries were supposed to offer closure, peace of mind, and reflection; instead I was nervous and suspicious. I talked to the ground where my mother's remains were said to be … I thought communing – you know, letting her know I was there – would make me feel better.

*Are you down there,* I'm wondering. I kept talking louder and louder, *Do you know I found you?* As I crouched talk-ing to my mother's grave, my heart was heavy with grief. I shouted, "Give me one sign!" When I looked up, there stood Mr. Chen.

"I worried when you rushed out of my office so I came to check on you. I'm sorry to interrupt your great homage to your ancestors."

I thanked Andrew Chen for his help. We exchanged smiles and went our separate ways.

To this day, I wonder if my mother is really buried there.

## A Night of Jazz with Gabriel and Sylvia

I hoped Gabriel's jazz gig would relieve me from the funk left from visiting the cemetery. I definitely needed a distraction.

When I arrived, James was entertaining Sylvia. Gabriel walked over and whispered, "Let's keep a secret today: the cousin thing. Tonight you're just a friend in town."

I thought, okayyyy, what's up with this?

I sat next to a lady named Anne May. Her late husband was a jazz musician – a drummer – and had owned Rossini's in Kitsalano for eighteen years. I wanted to tell Anne the truth about Gabriel. I got the feeling she wasn't convinced I was "a friend in town." But I kept my word.

The performance was fantastic. Sure enough, Gabriel – Gabe – was "a kickass horn player." I stayed 'til the end, and Gabriel and Sylvia gave me a ride to my hotel.

"Will we see you again before you leave?"

"As much as I'd love to, it will have to be another time … until we meet again."

## Walter Rae

I headed to the Port of Vancouver where I was meeting Walter Rae, a former pilot and tug master, aka "Vancouver's Clairvoyant."

When I asked for Walter Rae at some boat shed I was pointed in the direction of the docks. "Look for the boat named The Agent."

When I found it, I saw a man in white fishing boots, jeans and a worn out button-down squatting on deck looking out over the water.

"Walter Rae?"

As the man unfolded to standing he grinned, "That would be me."

His seaman's face was wind-weathered and he stretched out a calloused hand to help me aboard.

"It's a beautiful day for a boat ride; are you up for it?"

Over the sound of the motor and the whip of the wind, Walter talked about his job guiding ships to and from the sea while telling about his side work looking into unsolved murders. His list was long and impressive ...

The Murder of Janet Smith; 1924; The Babes in the Woods ... Jack the Ripper's killing spree in 1888 London ... the stories were grippingly eerie and I was spooked.

"It seems you live quite a diverse life – on one hand you're a sailor and the other you're a detective."

"I like truth. I like the work it sometimes takes to untangle the truth. And it's not about money or fame. I do it for the memory of the poor dead souls in hopes of bringing closure to their loved ones."

Hearing all of this was captivating – and a little frightening. But he hadn't asked a thing about me or why I was here.

We rode in silence for a bit. He stared at the water, minding the course.

"I've heard you're a seer of sorts?"

Diana and Walter Rae

He laughed. "Strangely enough for a sailor, yes, I'm the real deal. I know things, but I'm not sure why. Emotions come and go." Walter stopped the boat. "Let's see those pictures you've been talking about."

He looked at my mom: "She was gorgeous."

I showed the Castro brothers in Cuba, with the hunky mystery guy wearing trunks and shades in the background. "Do you have any idea who this could be?"

"Which Havana hotel is this?"

"Hotel Nacional de Cuba. This was taken in August of '59."

"Listen, if it was 1959, there was no mob stuff going on; Castro had closed the mob-run casinos and nightclubs by then. What I see in the photos is this: the guy in the trunks didn't ask to have his photo be taken. I think Castro asked."

"Oh. What are you implying?"

"Think about it. Did you ever know your father?"

"No, I'm still looking."

"I can tell you it's not any of these men. Your father died within the last thirteen months."

I was perplexed. "Do you believe my father was from Vancouver?"

"I don't. I believe he lived here and had connections – but he was an American."

Well. That 'insight' blew away all my aunts told me. According to them my father was most likely an Italian from Vancouver.

Back at the marina Walter moored the boat, I snapped some pictures, and he encouraged me to call if I ever wanted to talk more.

### Rick and Althea McCartie

After two and a half hours with Walter Rae, my next meeting was with Rick McCartie and his mother, Althea. Rick had told her my story, including the part about Parker Street, the address on my mom's Registration of Death. Althea was eight years older than Mom. I wondered aloud if she knew Donna.

"No, dear, but my husband might have. He was a musician and ran in the same circles. He was a lifeguard at the Crystal Pool; if she went there a lot, he would have known her for sure."

We drove around, unbeknownst to me, heading to Parker Street. Rick parked and Althea encouraged me … "Get out, dear. Go knock. If anyone answers, tell them it was your grandmother's house."

Rick and I headed to the door. Althea rolled her window down so she could clearly see and hear what went on. I knocked. There was no answer – until we were walking away and a lady opened the door. I turned around and said, "Excuse me, I know this may seem weird, but my grandmother once lived here, and I wondered if I might ask some questions."

"You don't have a Canadian accent," the lady accused.

Althea waved and called out, "It's true! This was her grandmother's house."

Once she heard Althea's accent, her attitude changed.

"My parents lived here since 1966, I bought the house from them. They have since moved on. Tom Needes has lived here since 1953; his house is that one." She pointed to the house "catty-cornered" from hers.

Rick and I looked at each other, crossed diagonally to the house and knocked. No answer. I put a note explaining the purpose of my visit, my card and Rick's number in an envelope and slipped it under the door.

Back at my hotel, I realized how tired I was. I declined Rick's offer for company, or dinner, thanking him profusely for all he had done, and gave him a big kiss …

"That's for you, my adventurous friend; thanks for making the week so exciting."

Today had left me wondering …

1.   Was Donna actually dead? Throughout this story, I never felt 100% sure she was dead.

2.   If so, was her body buried in the grave I had visited?

I am still searching for the truth behind the mystery of my birth mother.

## Chapter 34
### *Last Days in Vancouver*


Vancouver was having their 144th Labor Day celebration. The hotel was perfect for watching the world go by. The area was known as Hollywood North, the third-largest film industry site in North America, and I was psyched at the possibility of a celebrity sighting. I envisioned Julia Roberts, Owen Wilson, and Dolly Parton strolling by; rumors were they'd been in town the past few days.

The phone rang; it was Rick. "Where are you?"

"At the hotel, watching the festivities."

"Meet me out front in twenty. Let's go for a ride."

First he took me by Aunt Jan's old house in Burnaby. When I saw the state of it – or what was left of it – I cried out in shock. "What the? What happened?"

The lawn was nothing but weeds, the flowers all dead, the paint on the house faded and chipped, the once-bountiful garden withered and dried to the ground. I thought of Uncle Tom/Freddie buried there and thought, *poor Tom, someone will buy this house for the view and build condos on top of your grave; you will be the ghost on the hill.*

There was no answer at the door – and no signs of life, so we headed to Tom Needes' on Parker Street. With no luck at the front, I waited in the car as Rick went around back, and Tom opened the door.

"Hello, hello! You've caught me getting ready for a date,

but come on in. I've been expecting you both all day; my neighbor said you stopped by. Where's Diana?"

When I heard them talking, I walked to the back. Tom smiled and gave me a warm welcome. Pretty soon we were on a tour of his home.

"I've lived here since 1954."

"Did you know Grandmother?"

"Yes, I remember your grandmother. In those days I was always working, but I when I came home I'd see her out in the garden with a watering can. She grew prize-winning roses and often dropped off a bunch for our dinner table."

He didn't recognize Mom in my pictures, but remembered Dot. She had lived in this house for a while.

Tom excused himself to finish dressing for his date.

"I've never liked to keep a lady waiting." I would swear I saw a wink before we said goodbye.

Tomorrow was my last day and I had lots left to do. I was grateful to have had Rick and James with me that week; they helped keep my search on track. Looking back I felt this visit was a success but I had one more stop.

Over time I had been in contact with Detective Constable Daniel Murphy of the Major Crimes Homicide Unit at Vancouver's Police Department – our latest conversation had been only a week ago. After hearing my story, he had started an investigation into my mother:

### Subject: Request for Documents Regarding Donna Koloski Investigation

*Dear Diana,*
*I hope this email finds you well. I need a written statement or any documents you may have regarding the status of the investigation into your mother, Donna Koloski.*

*If you have evidence confirming you are Donna Koloski's daughter, please attach.*

*Thank you.*

*Best regards,*

*Detective Constable Daniel Murphy*

I sent all the information – letters, documents, photos – that I had so far.

I checked into the front desk that morning, confident I'd be able to meet with him, so what happened next was a rude surprise. It started when the front clerk asked how she could help me …

"Good morning. I'm here to speak with Detective Constable Daniel Murphy."

"Do you have an appointment?"

"No, I don't, but he's expecting me."

"Please take a seat. I'll see what I can do."

An officer emerged; it wasn't Detective Murphy.

"Hello, I understand you're here to see Detective Constable Daniel Murphy. You need an appointment. He won't be able to meet you without one."

"Can you please double-check? He's expecting me."

"Can you tell me more about your case?"

"Well, it happened back in 1967," I started …

"Forty-nine years ago," the officer mused. He shook his head and then added, "Do you know that every year, over 5,000 individuals go missing in Vancouver?"

"No, I didn't."

"Well, it's true. Like all of them, you need to fill out a police report and come back with an appointment."

I turned away. "What a jerk!" I tried not to stomp as I walked away, but I'm pretty sure all who were watching got the message that I wasn't pleased.

I thought: There's more than one way to handle this. I

headed straight for the library, took the elevator to the Special Collections Department and asked directions to the microfiche files. I searched for updates on home sales, found a record of Annie Kolosky (my grandmother), and the sale of the house on Parker Street in December 1966. I made copies and made haste to meet James for lunch.

It was no surprise to me to find Mr. Congeniality – James, of course – chatting with the hostess. He stopped and looked my way with concern.

"Are you okay? You seem out of breath. Your face is flushed."

"I'm fine, James. It's been a bit of a hectic morning." Right. I was still furious from being blown off at the police station.

"I'm all ears; let's hear it."

I shifted the focus. I was too frustrated to talk about the morning yet. "Tell me about the history of this hotel?"

"Well, it first opened its doors in 1927 ..." and he didn't stop "... I can easily picture your mom being a regular here during those days ..." – until we were seated – and he continued through lunch. It was a good distraction. Well played, James. He didn't seem to notice my haste to be on my way. Once we were alone in the car I felt calm enough to tell him about the morning.

"Diana, this doesn't feel right, the Parker Street location ... why would that address be on your mother's Registration of Death?"

"I have no idea. I assumed she lived in Montreal and died in May 1967."

"Hmmm. Your grandmother sold the house in the fall of 1966, and the paperwork was completed in December 1966. It seems fishy."

"Maybe Uncle Ron has more information."

"Then by all means, let's ask."

James stayed in the car while I knocked on the door and

waited. Uncle Ron opened the door, looking lost. At first he didn't seem to recognize me.

"Uncle Ron, it's Diana, your niece. I've been calling and leaving messages on your phone for days."

Ron seemed nervous. "You have to leave; you can't be here."

Out of nowhere, he inhaled deeply and shouted, "Years ago, Jan paid someone to scare you away! You know too much and ask too many questions! And the worst part? Jan stole from all of us!"

After he finished speaking he bent, putting his hands on his knees, and exhaled a long, long breath — as if he'd been holding all this in for so long that his body couldn't bear the weight of it.

The importance of this puzzle piece outweighed the shock as my mind put things in order. So, it was my aunt who was behind the killer's voice all these years? I couldn't believe it. But before I could say anything, my uncle begged me to leave.

"Please just GO!" he said, his voice trembling.

We did as asked and left to prevent the situation from escalating, and I felt a pang of sadness and compassion for Ron. I gave him a side hug and told him I loved him.

James spoke up, "I'm so sorry, my dear. It seems like we could both use a break."

We left; I suggested a cup of coffee. Of course Mr. Vancouver knew the perfect place. I told him after thinking about things, I should have known what my aunt's capabilities were from the very beginning, and that despite this latest rebuff, I had always had a wonderful time in Vancouver.

"Diana, you are from here. It's in your DNA," he said.

"James, my relationship with my family has been complicated from the beginning. I can survive anything they throw at me if I stay strong and keep a positive outlook. I'm not going to let anything stop me now; I've come such a long way and still have unresolved questions."

"What are they?"

"I want to know the truth about my mother. Is she dead? If she's not, then someone surely wants me to think otherwise. There's a Certificate of Death with her name on it and a grave, too."

"We'll figure it out. You are the most determined person I know. Walk away and try to process everything. It's your last night in town, and I'm making dinner: 8 o'clock sharp, my house. Rick will be joining us."

Before I left my room I stepped onto the balcony for a last view of the Vancouver spread beneath my window. I was definitely going to miss this view.

I picked up a bottle of Champagne for James's at the package store. I rang the doorbell. I could hear jazz playing and James fussing about in the kitchen through an open window.

"Hellooooo …"

"Come in, come in … welcome to my home … give me five minutes. Feel free to look around …"

His place was nice. It was decorated with soft lighting, lots of glass and soothing, rich hues. Dinner and drinks were served under twinkling white lights on the patio. We were popping the cork on the first bottle when Rick arrived with more. As we drank and laughed, I thought how I'd only known these two a short time but it felt like I was with old friends. Much to my surprise (and delight), James gave me a beautiful silk scarf. I told him it was too much (I recognized the designer), and he told me I was being silly and to wear it to work with his love.

James had been such help during my nine-day stay, attempting to contact anyone and everyone who might have known Mom. I felt fortunate to be leaving with so much information.

Around 1 AM Rick reminded me of our 4:30 AM date;

despite my protests (the hotel had bellhops, after all!), he insisted on coming by the hotel to help with my luggage.

I wrapped James in a heartfelt hug, whispering, "Cheers 'til next time."

Rick dropped me at my hotel. "I'll see you in a few hours …" and in what felt like a blink of an eye he was back, coffee in hand, and off we went to the airport in the dark. As the city lights faded in the rearview mirror, I told Rick, "Nine days wasn't enough."

"What's your hurry? You know you're welcome at my place."

The idea was tempting, but I knew my path led elsewhere – for now.

Rick insisted on carrying my luggage to the check-in area. I was grateful to have such a thoughtful friend and I felt the weight of our goodbye. We shared a hug, a promise to keep in touch and I nudged him playfully. "Hurry, before you get a ticket."

Settled on the plane, I opened my journal and took note of the adventures my quest had led me on so far – and the ones to come. I had visited places I never would have had it not been for the Donna Project – met incredible people, formed new family ties, and made great new friends. But now I was ready to be home, to see my son, and sleep in my own bed.

In Tampa David and his wife Erica met me at the airport.

"We followed you on Facebook."

They couldn't believe all the things I'd done, the many places I'd seen …

"David, it was an incredible experience. I can't wait to tell you everything."

# Chapter 35
## *Colorado Connections*

### A Tip from James

It was September; I was Colorado bound for a long weekend of research. Since spring I'd reached out to biological cousins from the Denver area – and there were plenty of them.

Two days before I left I heard from James. Through a series of texts, he revealed newly found information, namely:

1.   Joseph Gentile was the front man for Angelo Branca, a BC Supreme Court and Court of Appeals judge.

2.   The Bonanno family fled east and "mobbed up" in Vegas creating many interesting connections.

3. It seemed Basil Pantage was a decades-long fixture as a stock promoter, nightclub owner, and president of the annual Polar Bear swim that Barry Peacock attended every year.

James liked to throw hints before he cut to the chase – so I did some snooping and made notes of my own:

Jack Wasserman: A nightlife and celebrity columnist for Vancouver from 1949 to 1977.[12]

Angelo Branca: a 1930s Canadian middleweight boxing champ – as well as lawyer. He defended sixty-three people who faced murder charges – only one received capital punishment.[13]

### The Plane Ride to Denver
### Karen Schwimmer

The plane was half-full when we took off, and the passenger sharing my row was looking out the window. But the flight turned choppy – rough enough to rouse passengers and prompt my row-mate to introduce herself. "I'm Karen," she said. "I'm a frequent flyer, but this turbulence is making me nervous."

I started making small talk to try to ease her nerves and asked if she was going to Denver on vacation.

"No, I live there. Funny story, I went skiing one long weekend but never returned."

"Wow."

"Do you live in Denver?"

"No, I'm going to meet my family."

She looked at me, bewildered. "May I ask you a personal question?"

"Yes."

"By any chance are you adopted and meeting some family for the first time?" she asked gently.

"Well … it's complicated, but basically, yes."

"I was adopted and know nothing about my paternal biological family." Her voice was hopeful. "How did you find yours?"

I told her I used Ancestry and she admitted having an unopened kit at home.

"I stare at it every morning."

"You'll do it when you're ready."

We talked the entire flight. She had moved from the back to a better seat without asking and was convinced our sitting together was a sign. I told her about an Adoption Search Research Connection group in Denver, we swapped phone numbers and emails, and we promised to become friends on Facebook.

"I'm so glad I ran into you! Please, if you need anything while you're in town, call me!"

That evening Fran threw a small party just for me to meet my cousins at her home. John, Genevieve, Fran's adopted son, and his daughter Bonnie, who is Fran's granddaughter. It was a great evening; we talked about how we were related and my quest to find out who and how my biological dad was connected to the Route family. Fran had cooked a big Italian meal with desserts and drinks. I learned that my cousin, John, was certified and taught scuba diving. He also was single, and ex-Navy.

My cousin Genevieve had experienced multiple marriages, owned a pair of motorcycles, and loved to travel. Her charming nature, outgoing disposition, and enthusiastic eagerness to assist me made conversing with her a breeze.

Josh was adopted by Fran and her late husband, John Route. They have a wonderful granddaughter, living in the house to help Fran out.

Initially, I was nervous about meeting my cousins, but I had a blast and learned about my family. I turned in early that night and wrote in my journal that no matter what, I would never regret meeting them. I owed it to myself to learn about my family. "On a positive note, I gained a family and a few answers."

Cousins are essential members of my family. I reflected on my cousins, who I grew up with in New York. I will always treasure those memories. Those days were always filled with laughter and joy. While in Denver, I must show up and spend as much time as possible with my new family.

## Ilene and Ed Neues

Ilene, a dear friend from childhood lives in Denver with her husband Ed. It had been over forty years since we'd seen one another, and she was picking me up at Fran's for lunch. Meeting with an old friend felt good; it brought back many happy memories of summers as kids in Lake Peekskill, New York.

What a treat it was when I opened the door, and there was Ilene – we looked at each other and said, "You look the same. You haven't changed a bit." Then we laughed like always, and off we went to Cherry Creek Mall.

We were surprised it was already decked out for Christmas. The lights, decorations, and music made us feel festive and excited. We couldn't resist stopping at some of the boutiques and doing a little shopping.

During lunch, Ilene and I reconnected quickly. I'd forgotten how similar our personalities were. We share the same objectives and life values. It was a comfortable reunion. We reminisced about our wild times at Lake Peekskill and moved ahead; we were so happy to find that we still had plenty to share after all the years apart. We picked up right where we had left off.

**Fran Route** – My Denver hostess & family by marriage …

Fran Route wasn't a blood relative; her husband was. Their son John had found our connection through Ancestry; Fran contacted me in February 2016 and our friendship grew. That's how I ended up staying in her five-star-grade guest room.

## Davis Quint

David Quint was a Facebook friend I'd met after reading his narrative, *Father Unknown*. We shared stories about our individual journeys; David went first:

"Growing up I felt disconnected from my family, especially my father. I found out Dad came to the States from Switzerland as a child. I wanted to know more, so I helped him explore his past. On a trip to Switzerland we found the castle that turned out to be an orphanage."

After lunch, I left him to meet …

**Cousin Joanne and Ron** at their home …

Joanne and Ron were waiting at the front door.

"Come in, come in, it's cold out!"

"Hello! I'm Diana."

"Welcome! Let me get a good look at you." Joanne studied me and declared. "No doubt you have Route blood. No doubt at all."

I shared my story. Joanne and Ron had stories, too, with oodles of photos and names and connections – too many to keep up with – too much to comprehend. I took a deep breath, nodding my head, taking it all in. I simply wanted to enjoy this happy reunion.

**Writers Note:**

When my notes were sorted, my Denver family tree boiled down to:

Joanne is my cousin; her siblings were Clara and Virginia, Clara was Gabriel's mother.

Joanne and her husband, Ron have three sons – Eric, and twins, David and Daniel.

Gabriel, the 'kick-ass horn player' cousin in Vancouver contacted us while I was at his Aunt Joanne and Uncle Ron's house.

Fran stopped by and joined in the reunion. It did my heart good to see everyone getting along.

Joanne gave me a detailed copy of our family tree and vowed to order her DNA kit ASAP. "Everyone wants to help you, Diana!"

My time in Denver was packed with meetings like this. It was overwhelming.

All too soon, our time was over for the moment. As we approached the airport, my gut told me I would be back; I could feel more family secrets lurking.

# Chapter 36
## *My Florida Finale*

James Dubro wrote *Mob Rule: Inside the Canadian Mafia*. We became Facebook friends and agreed to meet. I reviewed my notes beforehand: he was a crime novelist, documentary producer, and investigative journalist with five best-selling novels.

I found him to be articulate, intelligent, and thoughtful, with an impressive education … Boston and Columbia Universities, graduate study at Harvard … he was currently teaching English lit at the University of Toronto.

My Vancouver connections posed the possibility my mother may have worked for the government. I dropped a few names … and James Dubro provided insights on who I might be dealing with and where to look for more information.

I could have listened to him all day. We used an iconic image of Marilyn Monroe as a prop for our farewell photo.

James DuBro, selfie by Diana

185

## Bruno

I was too wound up from my talks with James to be any good at work but I had to go back. Little did I know the surprise I'd find waiting for me.

I walked in the door and was immediately informed I had a guest. An older gentleman introduced himself as *Bruno*. I asked how he got my name.

"Through a friend. I was told you've been in jewelry for a long time, and I want a unique signet ring made … like one I saw in New York many years ago."

We went to my office; I closed the door and sat behind my desk. He settled into a seat across from me and began talking about his days in the New York Garment District.

Bruno leaned in, "I need to share an exciting story with you. One day, a man requested a custom pocket for a suit. He made it clear it wasn't for a wallet, explaining, 'It's for a concealed weapon.' From then on, he had my full attention. It was like I started leading a double life from that day on. Work and personal life I kept separate. I told no one about the people I became associated with."

"Then why are you telling me?"

"Because I feel you understand."

"But we've only just met."

"Things aren't always as they appear, Diana. I used to go on junkets with three hundred people to Havana. In '59, after Castro's rise and the mob's expulsion from Havana, we all moved to Vegas."

This one-sided conversation was weird; I wanted it to end. In less than two hours this stranger had told me dark secrets he insisted he'd never even told his family! Hoping to wrap things up, I stood, thanked him for sharing such an incredible story and tried to see him out. Instead he kept his seat and looked at me intently.

"There's more."

I sighed inwardly and sat back down.

"Listen. Life is interesting. I've seen how the other side lives."

Bruno talked about lunches with an associate named Anthony Scotto who generously handed out hundred-dollar bills wherever he went.

He went on about 'significant meetings with police chiefs, District Attorneys, and various United Auto Workers from both the States and Canada …'

When Bruno did decide to leave, we exchanged business cards. When he was gone, my boss asked whether the gentleman in the suit made a significant purchase.

I chuckled to myself and answered, "I'm working on it."

On the way home, I called Steve. I was so unnerved by Bruno's surprise visit that I ended up at his house, trying to talk things through and slept in his guest room; I didn't feel safe going home alone.

When we arrived at Ilene and Ed's the next day, the snow had piled up in the driveway. The weather in Denver became the topic of conversation. "The snow melts quickly on the roads. Temperatures can swing from 25 to 80 degrees in just a few hours. You'll see snow on the ground and people in short sleeves walking around. The summers are hot and dry, despite the low humidity; your skin can burn in seconds from the sun's intensity."

My convertible was completely enveloped in snow, with the Florida license plate prominently visible. I asked Ed, "When did my car arrive?"

"Yesterday."

Inside, I settled in and told Ed and Ilene that I would start looking for a place closer to my employment the next day. Later in the evening, Steve called.

"Hi Diana, I know you've just arrived, but I have sad news. Brent's mother passed away today."

"Oh, Steve. I'm at a loss for words. I'm so sorry. I had hoped she had more time and had been praying for a miracle.

Please send me the details—my love to Brent, his family, and you. We'll talk soon. Love you."

"I love you too," Steve said.

My tears wouldn't stop. I realized I had never expressed to Steve's partner, Brent Corbie, how much his mother, Phyllis, meant to me. Death is a complex and unfathomable reality, and we all navigate through it differently. I remembered Phyllis, how she beamed with pride for all her children. But above everything, she cherished her relationship with her son, Brent.

## Life Goes On

Over the years of traveling, researching, and meeting new friends new family, other facets of my life had moved along. David had grown into a handsome, thoughtful young man and was married to a beautiful woman named Erica.

And I was gradually losing my job.

Over the past four months, I'd received two pay cuts. Rumor had it the Tampa office was closing. As a result of the downsizing, I applied to another company and scheduled an interview for a new position – in Denver. I aced the interview and was offered the Denver job. I asked for a few days to consider. I thought of how a move to Denver would impact my loved ones – and me. In the end I threw caution to the wind and accepted the offer.

The evening before my flight out to Colorado I had dinner with David. Erica was away on business. He knew about my job situation. He knew I wasn't happy living in Clearwater anymore. He knew I needed change.

What I don't think he realized was how important it was to me … finding my identity – I don't know that I fully understood it either. He walked me to my car and we hugged for a long moment. I wept as I drove away.

A car service took me to the airport, then up, up and away! I was off to a brand new life.

# Chapter 37
## *The Manchester*

My VW convertible arrived in Denver days before I did and was already coated with snow; only the Florida plates showed. I had rented a fantastic place in the Wyman Historic District less than ten-minutes from work. It was tastefully furnished with the basics, and I unpacked and arranged personal touches and made the new space feel like home.

I bought passes for the local botanical gardens and art museum, registered at the Denver Genealogy Library, and became a regular cyclist in a nearby park. Everything was going great until my new job was suddenly in peril; the Denver location changed management, and the new manager brought his own team. I was offered some obligatory alternatives – none as good as my original position – and I declined, knowing fate had sent me to Denver for more reasons than a job.

I became a member of Adoption Search Research Connection (ASRC) and attended monthly meetings at Montview Boulevard Presbyterian Church. Most members had known each other for years. Being the new kid in town, I felt a little left out, but that didn't stop me from joining the conversation – after all, we were all adoptees.

I was captivated by others' unique journeys. As I shared my own, I sensed sincere interest and empathy as we sat in a horseshoe sharing research and stories. I had found a place I could learn and grow, surrounded by kind-hearted individuals with good intentions. I had found my tribe.

Fresh perspectives enriched my story and I met new people – like Stacey Sanders. Stacey was the force behind Elevating Connections, an organization dedicated to supporting foster children and former youth in foster care. Together, we took part in Elevating Connections' events and attended Jewish services during the holidays.

My first Ancestry meeting at the Central Library was attended by people of all ages.

I lucked out by sitting next to Bonnie Garramone. Even at eighty-seven years of age, her work was far from finished. When it came to Italian genealogy, Bonnie was the authority and her expertise extended well beyond Denver. She was impressed with how much I'd accomplished, nicknaming me "Sleuth." In two hours of conversation, I learned a tremendous amount about my family and tips about tracing my roots.

"You don't want to scare anyone away. Any older person who is willing to talk should be handled with kid gloves," Bonnie advised. "I ran across a few notes scribbled down while I was putting my folders away, and I'm going to send them and others to you. Every note is important."

The free time I had for research was great, but I kept my eye out for employment opportunities, too. I had been out cycling and stopped for coffee when I noticed a huge banner advertising, "Teachers Needed" in front of a Goddard school. I was a licensed teacher so I went home, changed, and walked in without an appointment. The owners, Elizabeth and Martin Meier, and the director Heather Hartmann welcomed me warmly.

I took an application home and interviewed the next day; I started a few days later. Within six weeks, I had Colorado teaching credentials. I started as a lead teacher and was soon promoted to front office administrative assistant. I loved it at the Goddard School and knew I wouldn't return to retail.

When I wasn't working I explored Denver. I discovered the historic lower downtown district where my Route ancestors were known for their fresh produce stand. I spent time with cousins, learning family history. On weekends, I was with family or friends, attending various events. Throughout the year, I explored the mountains and surrounding cities. I researched synagogues and spoke to a Rabbi. I invested in a good bike helmet and rode with my camera, photographing historic homes.

As I wandered my neighborhood streets, I drifted in time, imagining life in the 1920s and 1930s … I could almost hear horses' hooves pulling carriages along cobblestoned paths …

# Chapter 38
## *Dermod Travis*
## *A Connection Through Vancouver*

On Monday, August 7, 2017 I received my first email from Dermod Travis in Canada.

His credentials were solid: He was affiliated with Integrity BC, an organization founded to help restore accountability to British Columbia's politics. He trusted the source that had led us together and was convinced I, too, was genuine – thus our long correspondence began.

At first I was skeptical, but over time I grew comfortable with Dermod. His selflessness and persistence were exactly what I needed. I shared the photos of Donna, recounted her two-week holiday in 1959 Cuba, and, of course, I showed the photo of Castro and Raul with the mystery man. Dermod confirmed the identities of Raul and Castro. I told him my mother took the pictures and asked his thoughts about the man in the middle being Errol Flynn.

*Diana,*

*It's possible Errol Flynn could be the man pictured between Castro and Raul, but confirming his identity needs closer examination. If you have any more details about the photo let me know.*

*Given the timing of your mother's visit to Cuba, its likely intelligence agencies had her on a watchlist. While I'm skeptical*

192

*about the Royal Canadian Mounted Police (RCMP) retaining those files – or sharing them, it's worth asking.*

*Archives Canada might have documents that are presumably declassified by now. Have you reached out to McGill University regarding her status and records?*

*- Dermod*

I responded, same as always, that I had tried, unsuccessfully, to access McGill University's files on Donna, but without official proof of being her daughter, I had no rights.

Dermod used his resources to investigate that era in Vancouver and Montreal, but because Canada did not have CSIS, (today's Canadian counterpart to the CIA), back then, it was a long shot. The intelligence work fell to the RCMP.

When Dermod asked if my mother's data was thoroughly scrubbed, I told him I was pretty sure it had been.

That's when he asked if I'd be willing to speak to the media and we made plans to arrange a meeting when I was in Vancouver over Christmas, 2018.

Dermod continued emailing websites of interest and we maintained contact, sharing what we learned. I was grateful for his commitment to help me and answered all the questions I could.

When asked for details about Mort Shulman, I gave him contact details for Mort's lawyer, Henry Abbott, the immigration attorney who was threatening to deport me. Dermod found Mort's son, Samuel, and discovered two locations my mother might have gone. The first was Ben Ash in Montreal, and the second is Yangtze Restaurant on Van Horne. I gave my consent to Dermod to investigate on my behalf and checked my email daily in anticipation. One link took me to a story that sounded all too familiar:

*"CBC Investigates: How one man's search for Quebec adoption records turned into a 'wild goose chase …' Ken Waisanen,*

*an adoptee, is trying to find his birth father and any relevant medical history."*

Dermod nut-shelled the lengthy article:

*'Waisanen applied to Quebec for his adoption record but was told it's a complicated process. There is no central registry for adoptions in Quebec, so an adoptee must know where they were born and then apply to the child and family services author-ity. Waisanen's application was sent to the wrong agency several times, and he had to start over from scratch a year after his quest began.'* [14]

I didn't hear from Dermod for almost two months; mean-while I prepared a letter to Canadian Prime Minister Justin Trudeau and sent it to Dermod for feedback.

The letter I sent to Prime Minister Justin Trudeau is sum-marized below:

*Dear Prime Minister Trudeau,*

*My name is Diana K. Hochberg. I have been on a journey that has spanned the last twenty-four years; I am on a quest to uncover my family history in Vancouver, British Columbia.*

*Throughout this time, efforts have involved respected journal-ists, socialites, authors, and archivists in both Canada and the United States.*

*I am currently in communication with Dermod Travis, an affiliate of Integrity BC as he tries to assist in my search. Despite extensive efforts, insurmountable obstacles have prevented suc-cess and my mother's records appear to have vanished, leaving a significant part of my life shrouded in mystery.*

*I was born in Canada in the mid '50s. Under arrangements made by Mort Shulman, I was taken from Canada and placed with a Jewish family in the United States. This transfer was con-ducted without legal adoption procedures, making me a 'black-market baby.' Mort Shulman later confessed to committing a felony through his actions.*

*I write to you seeking not just answers but closure. I am Canadian by birth, and firmly believe understanding one's heritage is a fundamental right. My Canadian birthright is a part of who I am, and gaining insight into my mother's story is crucial for my sense of identity and peace of mind.*

*Any assistance or guidance that will uncover my mother's records, reveal the circumstances of my adoption, and show the way for me to officially claim my Canadian heritage would be invaluable. I yearn for closure and the opportunity to fully embrace my Canadian roots.*

*I appreciate your consideration and look forward to the possibility of your support in this deeply personal matter.*

*Sincerely,*

*Diana K. Hochberg*

I was relieved when Dermod responded:

### Subject: Letter to Prime Minister Justin Trudeau

*Diana,*

*The letter is quite good.*

*I've been working on two projects at the same time. Once you arrive in Vancouver, I'd like to discuss your holiday plans with you and meet with Daphne Bramham. Please share the address of your West End lodging.*

*- Dermod Travis*

# Chapter 39
## *Winter Break 2018*

I had planned to celebrate the New Year with Gabriel in Vancouver but several months earlier, Barry Peacock had invited me to stay with him. When I got to Barry's it was 4:00 AM, so I put my bags beside the couch, grabbed the pillow and blanket he'd left, and crashed until 10:00 AM. I opened the drapes to a breathtaking city view, but inside, the morning sun illuminated a different story altogether. I looked around and was shocked at the neglect. There wasn't even coffee.

I changed clothes, called Rick and we met at a café nearby. Just as I was reveling in how lovely it was to catch up with an old friend, he asked an odd question:

"Did you ever wonder whether your mother is still alive and living in the West End?"

"What makes you think that's even conceivable?"

"I believe in Christmas miracles." And he stopped at that.

I brushed it off and we went shopping, checking out all the decorations around town. The shops were crowded and everyone was full of holiday spirit.

Back at Barry's I was preparing for Gabe's performance at the Blue Martini when Barry begged out of going, claiming he needed to rest.

"Is there anything else I can do for you?"

"No, just leave." Barry was not at all himself.

I took a cab to the bar, where Gabe greeted me with a smile. I had a great seat for his sold-out performance, met his friends and fellow musicians. After an outstanding evening, Gabriel dropped me off at Barry's.

I awoke on Christmas morning to a silent apartment, and Barry deeply asleep. When he awoke I asked if the sleep had helped.

"Yes, I needed it. I'll take medicine before we go out later."

For the next hour we talked about Mom. Barry reminded me of his offer to use his Montreal connections to help me, but warned it could be dangerous. I was perplexed; why would there be a problem after all these years?

"Let me look into it. In the meantime, it's Christmas and we have reservations at the Park Pub restaurant in English Bay." Over dinner, we talked about how Christmas was different for children growing up Jewish and he asked if I had a favorite holiday movie.

"It's usually a toss between *Miracle on 34th Street* and *It's a Wonderful Life*. This year is different. I want a Christmas Miracle. I want the Prime Minister of Canada to grant me my Canadian birthright."

Barry drank continuously during dinner, and his speech became mean. I chalked his behavior up to mixing cold meds and alcohol – and said so. Something didn't feel right. He wasn't himself, and though I wanted to be a good friend, when he went nuts in the crowded restaurant, screaming at me to shut up – I paid my tab and left.

I was gone early the next morning, leaving a goodbye note that said: "I'll call you in a few. You need to get your act together. Take care."

I checked into the Blu Horizon hotel, took a long hot shower and slept hard. I awoke refreshed, and made plans with James for a late lunch at our favorite Chinatown restaurant. He wondered what I was doing on that end of town; I told him it was a long story and we left it at that.

Being with James cheered me up, and our conversation drifted.

"I am determined to find someone who knew your mother. She'd only be eighty, you know. There must be someone in this town that knew her. I want you to see Dad again, so we can work together."

The next day James and I visited his dad. I was sad to see his health had declined but was glad to see his smile. We had lunch and caught up, then went our separate ways.

I was meeting my friend, Mark at a coffee shop in Yaletown. I drove through the crappy weather to meet Mark and greeted him with a smile and a soggy handshake – I'd left my umbrella at the hotel. We laughed for a few minutes about me being drenched and unprepared for the weather, then launched into a conversation that lasted several hours. Mark was an exciting guy and a free spirit, and there was chemistry between us. But I didn't have time to indulge – I was on a mission. We left the coffee shop for a pub around the corner.

"Diana, I know your mother's story and the people in North Vancouver. Let me investigate further and see what I can find out. I know an old-timer who worked the ski slopes in Canada and Europe way back in those days. There's a chance he might remember your mother."

The weather continued to be awful as I tried to catch up on my research. I finally made it to the library to read up on the rights of a black-market baby born in Canada and reared in the States. Though I had little success, I did find a new address for Aunt Dot.

Out the window snow fell in large, heavy flakes. Only moments later, the entire city appeared covered in a white blanket. I called Rick to see what time we were meeting for dinner. We arrived at the same time. He looked handsome in suit and tie. We discussed New Year's Day and planned to go to North Vancouver for a party. We closed down the restaurant at 3 AM.

Gabriel's New Year's Eve performance was sensational and the party was full swing a few hours past the stroke of midnight. It was wonderful to be welcoming the New Year in Vancouver with family and new friends.

We spent New Year's taking in the town's celebrations, wandering around until we were lost in the city ... grabbing a late afternoon coffee ... going to my friend Francine's annual New Year's Day party ... and ended up back at his place talking about any and everything until 5 AM when Rick made coffee and we made our way out of the house and on to the airport where we said our farewells, once again ...

"You know, this seems to be becoming a habit."

I turned around and hugged him ... "Come to Denver?"

"Let me think about that."

# Chapter 40
## *Winter Letters in Denver*

After Vancouver the New Year was off to a good start. I resumed writing, accepted a director's position at work, enrolled in online courses – and had an email from Dermod Travis.

It was about Errol Flynn and the summer of '59. Flynn was at the Hotel Nacional de Cuba the same time as my mother. There were time-stamped YouTube videos to prove it. Three months after the videos, Errol Flynn died.

And my friend Barry Peacock was found dead in his apartment. The sad news set me back. Barry had been helping with my research through his Montreal contacts.

I thought about how far I'd come since my first DNA test in 2015. I could have stopped after I found my mother's family. What more did I need to know? I sighed. Yes, I had come far … but loose ends dangled …

… Take the letter I sent to Prime Minister Justin Trudeau: it'd been months since I sent it. I'd been so busy, I failed to follow up. As if my thoughts had conjured it, February fifth's mail contained a letter from the Prime Minister's Ottawa office. It was clearly a form letter – automatically dispatched to queries such as mine. I had so hoped my letter would have an impact, especially considering Margaret Sinclair Trudeau, PM Trudeau's mother, was a Vancouver native. The letter politely acknowledged the receipt of my letter and directed me to a website. An "Executive Correspondence Officer" signed it. I was mightily disappointed. Did the Prime Minister even read my letter? Despite my efforts to persuade him, I wasn't making any progress

The next week I had a number of emails from Ancestry, including a message from one Eric Teague. His words piqued my interest, so I called him that evening.

When he answered, he said, "I still don't understand how we're related."

"I checked my family tree and found that Dustin Overmyer and Stephanie are related to both of us."

Eric had several conversations with Stephanie, and a DNA test confirmed her grandfather was Kenneth Teague, my half-uncle.

"Diana, this is amazing. Stephanie is my cousin, and Kenneth is our great-uncle Kenny. Ruby Pauldino, Kenny's mother, is also your grandmother and my great-grandmother."

Our interest shifted to Pauldino family history. Ruby Pauldino had been married several times, and she played a significant role in the puzzle of my paternal lineage. Her first husband was Daniel Pauldino, Sr., son of Michael Pauldino and Antonette Route. Voila! I'd found the puzzle piece that connected me to the Route family.

"Diana, if Daniel and Ruby are your grandparents, then you're on your way to finding your biological father. Ruby and Daniel had three

Grandmother Ruby Pauldino

children together: two boys, Daniel and Michael, and one girl, Darlene Jeanette."

Our relationship flourished and my journey took on new life. We found several Denver addresses for Ruby Wilkinson Pauldino Teague. Ruby married Daniel Pauldino in 1924; she was seventeen, he was twenty-five.

Motivated, I drove to two addresses where my grand-mother had once lived. The first had been torn down and replaced with a modern structure.

That evening there was an email from Canada's Ministerial Enquiries Division regarding the letter I had sent to Prime Minister Trudeau. It turned out to be another automatic re-sponse – via email – acknowledging my correspondence and telling me things I'd learned already.

*"... In general, persons born in Canada and those born abroad to a Canadian parent have a claim to Canadian citi-zenship ...*

*Once an application is received, a citizenship officer who as-sesses the applicant's particular circumstances reviews it. If the person is a Canadian citizen, a citizenship certificate is issued. If the person is not a Canadian citizen, a letter explaining how to obtain Canadian citizenship is provided.*

*We hope that this information is helpful.*

*Sincerely,*

*B. Lapointe*

*This electronic address is not available for a reply.*

It was clear my original letter to the Prime Minister hadn't been given the courtesy of a reading.

I was so tired of being thwarted that I felt like throwing in the towel.

But I couldn't. I'd come so far ...

# Chapter 41
## *Gaetano's & the Pauldinos*

When Dermod and I reconnected I had much to share. I'd identified my paternal grandparents, their two sons and a daughter. I gave him the basics – names, dates – I could hear the clicks of a keyboard as he searched ...

"It looks like they moved a lot ... between Denver, Vancouver, British Columbia, Seattle, and Las Vegas ... and this has gone on for years. I'm seeing signs of mafia affiliations."

"Do you have any police connections, Dermod? I'd like to find some pictures. I think I'm close to finding my father; he's either Daniel Pauldino, Jr. or Michael Pauldino. Eric and I discovered their mother, Ruby Pauldino, had mob ties. My Denver cousins don't have a clue about the Pauldinos."

My research into the Smaldone family left me with a lot of questions. Even though it was plain they dabbled on the wrong side of the law (all the way back to the 1920s), their community support had been solid for a hundred years ... as far back as Prohibition, they were equally infamous criminals and honored humanitarians.

Brothers Clyde and Checkers Smaldone had owned and operated Gaetano's Italian Restaurant since 1947 in northwest Denver. It was the base of their mob empire.

I found this interesting tidbit in the Denver Library:

*"Many people said Eugene "Checkers" Smaldone was 'a playful man who liked to put on 'impromptu one-man opera performances.'"* [15]

Well. I guess even gangsters had a playful side.

And I came across an article in the magazine *5280-Mile-High Magazine*:

*Things You Didn't Know About Gaetano's:*

*The iconic, onetime mob restaurant turns 70 – and you can party there all weekend.*

*The Smaldone underworld enterprise died, but Gaetano's didn't.*

*Frank Sinatra and Sammy Davis Jr. both played high-stakes card games at Gaetano's.*

*The Restaurant Is Haunted.*

*Al Capone visited the restaurant once; in the '40s and '50s the Smaldones were buying whiskey from Canada – until they found it cheaper from a guy in Chicago – a guy named Al Capone.* [16]

I was intrigued. I went to Happy Hour at Gaetano's on a Saturday. It was February. I cozied up to the bar and was greeted with a friendly smile from the bartender. I ordered a mimosa.

"You don't look like a mimosa girl. Let me surprise you. It's on me if you don't like it."

I love a great bartender, and this guy was on the money. The cocktail Paul made was much better than a mimosa. I sipped my new favorite drink and looked around; it was like a time warp from the '40s.

"Does anyone from the old days still come here?"

Paul chuckled. "Oh, yeah … but you're way too early. Come back tonight after eleven. I'll introduce you to a few of the old-timers." As I finished my drink, Paul promised to save a seat if I came back later. I giggled as I walked out – the front doors were bulletproof!

Back in the car I had a call from Eric. "What's going on? I've become obsessed with genealogy. I'm addicted! But I'm confused about DNA 'segments.' What are they, anyway?"

I promised to help him understand DNA segments. And I told him about Gaetano's and that I was going back. Oh, how he wished he could join me. Maybe another time, kiddo.

I was back at Gaetano's before eleven. The smell of fresh pasta and melting cheese wafted through the air, a scent from my childhood. A seat at the bar was open. I ordered the clams casino appetizer and a glass of cabernet.

A gentleman from the other end of the bar approached. He had a friendly smile and warm eyes. Speaking softly, he said, "I understand you have questions. I'm Lorenzo; with whom do I have the pleasure of speaking?"

"My name is Diana. I'm looking for information about my family tree. I believe some of my relatives were regulars here."

"Look around; Smaldone family portraits and newspaper articles cover the walls … I've been coming here since I was a child. Do you have names in mind?"

"My DNA test says I'm related to the Smaldones; I'm looking for information on the Pauldino brothers."

"Ahhh, come with me. I have something to show you," he said, gently grabbing my hand and whispering, "We're going into the men's room."

"I am not going into the men's room with you!"

Hearing my fuss, the manager walked over and assured me everything would be okay. I thought, what the hell? I've said there was no going back and, truth be told, I was feeling a little gutsy.

And off to the men's room I went.

In a bar I'd been to once.

With a man I'd just met.

The door was styled in classic gangster, and led to a room with the FBI logo and the Smaldone family's connections mapped out over the walls. I pulled out my phone and snapped pictures, I recognized some names ... Bridwell, Bonnano, LoSasso – and Michael Pauldino, which stood out the most.

Lorenzo stared at me. "He's your father?"

"No! Well, I don't know."

Back at the bar Lorenzo announced to the entire restaurant, "Her father is Michael Pauldino! He's on the FBI's most-wanted wall."

Laughing, I said, "Stop it."

The manager came over and told me to "Order whatever you want; your dad is on the wall."

"I'm not 100% sure; it's a fifty-fifty chance."

Several people came to congratulate me for my dad being one of the FBI's most wanted.

At this point, I needed another drink. And I had more questions for Lorenzo.

"Is there anyone else here tonight who knows the Pauldino family?"

"Let me ask; I'll be back."

A lady walked over and asked for my autograph. Confused, I asked why?

"Your dad was a legend."

Lorenzo was back, asking about Mom. I pulled out her picture and told him her name was Donna Kole. "She was a Vancouver native."

He froze. "Does she ski?"

"Yes."

"I've seen her here. I was young ... but once or twice, I've seen that woman here."

"Are you certain?"

"Yes. I wouldn't forget a face like hers. Michael visited Canada often; did you know that?"

I had just learned about the Pauldino brothers; and hadn't shared this part of my story with Lorenzo. All these years

I thought my aunts and Doris Langerak were referring to the Petrillo brothers when it was the Pauldino brothers from Denver instead. Aunt Jan described the Petrillo brothers as wealthy Italians living in North Vancouver.

I asked about Lorenzo's family and their connections to Denver.

"I wish my dad were alive; he would have so much to tell. Meanwhile, I'll ask around." It was 2:00 AM, the kind of late night where time feels suspended. We captured the moment in photos, exchanged numbers with promises to stay in touch, and then I headed for home. As I walked away, the iconic strains of Frank Sinatra's "My Way" drifted through the air, a hauntingly perfect anthem for the crossroads I didn't yet know I was approaching.

A few weeks passed, and I was walking in the botanical gardens as I mulled over whether to stay in Colorado or return east when my phone disturbed my musings …

I didn't know the number but answered anyway. Looking back, maybe I shouldn't have. It was my first encounter with Sofia, who claimed she was Michael Pauldino's daughter.

She asked if I'd like to meet downtown that afternoon at four. Sure, it was spur of the moment, but …

A young lady was waiting outside the coffee shop … she was my height, our hair the same color … and as she lifted her gaze and smiled – the resemblance was uncanny – we shared the same skin tone and eye shape – it was as if I was seeing myself at thirty-five.

Sofia felt it, too. I could see the shock; she couldn't stop staring.

A cheerful waiter spouting the daily specials broke the spell. We ordered coffee and croissants and I started talking. I gave her the run-down of my story and launched into how I'd ended up here, with her – it was all a matter of DNA testing.

"Sofia, I know this must be overwhelming for you. I've

been dedicated to this research for so long that these details are old hat – but every new piece of the puzzle brings new questions. I'm now wondering if my grandmother was Ruby Pauldino. How can she be yours, too?"

"Wait a minute. I know my grandmother married several times, isn't it possible you might actually be my cousin?"

We talked about our families – mothers, fathers, their mothers and fathers, aunts and uncles, cousins once, twice, and three times removed – trying to figure out connections. To say the least it was confusing.

Then I mentioned Vancouver.

"Vancouver!" Sofia fell silent and cast her eyes downward. When she finally looked up, she said "Daddy and Uncle Danny adored Vancouver. Dad often reminisced that his first true love was from Canada, and described it as a magical place. He always hoped to show me."

I sensed Sofia's confusion; this was hard for her. "Sofia, it was in the 1950s when your dad and Danny went to Vancouver. Tell me about yourself."

"Mom and Dad met in Vegas. I have a brother, Luca. Your cousin Eric's cousin, Stephanie, sent me a DNA Ancestry kit. I agreed to take it – I grew up with only a few relatives and no cousins, so I'd love to know about more family – but I'm terrified!"

"I understand. My son, David and his wife, Erica, live in Florida. I also have a stepdaughter, Claire Marie, who lives in Germany."

We talked about our lives, careers, and families for a few hours. I was excited but uncertain at the same time. It felt odd to have such a connection with a stranger.

We left the restaurant, and Sofia asked for a ride to her apartment. She talked about her time in the service, how she returned home from the Marines with severe PTSD, which disrupted her return to civilian life, ended her marriage and left three children in foster care.

My intuition waved a BIG RED FLAG, and I hesitated going to her apartment. But she insisted on doing her DNA test and sending it off and she didn't want to do it alone. I helped her with the paperwork while she took the test. All the while we continued to talk about the possibility that we were cousins.

"Mom won't be happy either way," she mumbled.

"Your dad didn't cheat on your mom; it happened before they met. If it is Danny, he wasn't married at that time either. Sofia, I had a wonderful father. I'm not looking for a new one. I simply want to know family history."

As usual, my intuition was right on, because a few days later, a hysterical Sofia called, screaming and yelling.

"Diana, you forced me to take that DNA test! You destroyed my life!" She was sobbing.

I hung up. She sent ten-plus text messages loaded with foul language … she was furious.

Her abusive texts continued; I had no choice – I blocked her from my phone and social media platforms.

Without me to vent to, Sofia proceeded to go nuts on my cousins, and they, too, blocked her. I had to cut ties with her, family or no. I had no interest in pursuing contact with her – or anyone – in that state of mind.

Eric understood but he really was hooked on our history now and had gone so far as to locate Luca's email and send him a long message:

### Subject: Shared Family History

*Hello Luca,*

*My name is Eric Michael Teague. Some months ago I met Diana Hochberg, who has been on a quest to confirm her biological roots. After much research and a DNA test that led her to me, I submitted a DNA test and the results have led me to you. The test indicates I'm your cousin.*

*I'm aware this is a lot to take in. Diana is a close cousin and is incredible. I have been working with her to figure out our biological connection. If you're interested, I'm sure she'd be willing to help sort things; she's been researching for years and knows a great deal about DNA testing.*

*Anything you want to know, I will answer.*
*I hope to hear from you,*
*Eric Teague*

I followed up Eric's email with one of my own …

### Subject: Discovering Our Shared Roots

*Luca,*
*I'm sure you have many questions.*
*As Eric explained, I have been on a years-long search to find my biological roots. Of course there is more to the story.*
*The bottom line is that I value family, and if I have any family that I don't know of, I want them to know I exist.*
*Ask me anything. I'll do my best to explain.*
*Sincerely,*
*Diana*

### Subject: Re: Discovering Our Shared Roots

*Diana,*
*It is a lot to take in. I tried to follow the timeline, but it's complicated.*
*I know very little about my father's parents. My dad was Michael Eugene Pauldino (1926–2015), a native of North Denver. His parents were Ruby and Daniel. Michael had a brother,*

*also named Daniel, and a sister named Darlene. He married my mother, Nina Carnes, they had me in 1981.*

*My sister was born in 1983. Our dad was twenty years older than Mom. Uncle Danny and Auntie Darlene each had one child. Danny has a daughter named Cheryl, who must be close to sixty. Darlene has a son named Mario, who is going to be fifty-nine.*

*That is all I know,*
*Luca.*

Luca verified everything we knew about his dad, uncle, and aunt.

### Subject: Family Info

*Hi Eric,*
*Sofia started taking drugs in 2008; I haven't spoken to her since. I'm married and have two children. Sofia has either three or four kids. I've never met any of them.*
*Luca*

Eric and I spoke on the phone that night after work.

"Eric, after all the drama with the Pauldinos, I've decided to cut communications with them. I thought Luca would be interested to meet me, but apparently that's not the case. I remember how it ended with Sofia – with tears and a sense of loss."

"I am so sorry I talked you into meeting her."

"Eric, stop. It's okay. In less than a month I'm headed back to the East Coast. I want to spend my time left here with my family and friends who truly care. It's good to know the truth about your identity and family history – even if it means you can't have a relationship with them. I now know who I am. I've come to realize this is their loss."

# Chapter 42
## *Leave-the-Door-Open Road Trip*

Moving back to the east coast at the end of April left a whole month to pack and prepare. My inbox overflowed with messages from colleagues, wishing me well. I was humbled; I hadn't realized the impact I'd made. I wrote a note to each individual.

My friend Grace and I hadn't found the time to say our goodbyes at work, so we met for lunch. We talked about our families and promised to stay in touch – and we have to this day. During our conversation, I mentioned my book project and Grace shared a deeply personal part of her life – she grew up in foster care but was fortunate to be adopted by a wonderful woman. Meanwhile my Ancestry mailbox overflowed with requests from new cousins eager to connect. I tried to answer every message – I remembered how it felt to reach out and hear nothing.

I was meeting a cousin, Lisa Shannon, on Sunday. A mutual cousin, Colleen Fisher, had introduced us on social media. Colleen, originally from Denver, now lived in Arizona, and Lisa was visiting from Turkey. Lisa made me feel at ease immediately. She was thrilled to hear I was writing a book about my experience and thanked me for letting her be a part of my journey.

As the saying goes, parting became such sweet sorrow.

I attended my last Adoption Search Research Connection

(ASRC) meeting on April 24 at Montview Boulevard Pres-byterian Church. I couldn't believe it had been a year since I joined. The people were amazing and honest; I would miss each one. Denver News 9 came to our meeting that night and taped a segment titled "Storytellers: Adoptees share se-crets, search for family. An adoption support group tries to reunite adoptees with their biological family."[17]

Despite different stories, we all wanted the truth. I shared the story and a picture of my grandmother, Ruby Wilker-son Pauldino, and shared my experience in Denver that led me to believe my potential father was either her son Danny Pauldino or Michael Pauldino. I certainly couldn't leave out the odd anecdote that they were something akin to modern-day Robin Hoods.

My brother Jesse flew in from Philadelphia the next day for the drive back east.

We set out early the next morning.

Destination: Pawleys Island, SC – "Where Happy People Live"

We followed I-70 through Kansas, spent the night in Mis-souri and crossed the Mississippi River the next day, headed south toward Nashville on I-40.

All those miles gave us time to talk, and we talked about our upbringing. It was the first time we'd ever talked about his adoption. He had disturbing memories of Ethel's strug-gle with obsessive-compulsive disorder (OCD). In chilling detail, Jesse described being regularly beaten with a belt. I vividly remember the welts on his skin and how he made up excuses for them; now I knew he was shielding me.

When Jesse was seventeen, he persuaded Daddy to sign pa-pers allowing him to join the Army. Jesse's departure left me to cope with Ethel's erratic behavior alone. I often found myself hiding under the bed or the dining table to avoid her rage, but she always managed to drag me out by my feet. Before Dad was home from work, Ethel would wash my mouth out with soap and scrub my skin until it turned red, all in an obsession to "eliminate all the germs." As soon as Daddy was home, Ethel would make herself out as a loving wife with perfect children. We never told our father the truth. Ethel was diagnosed with terminal cancer when I was nine. Nineteen months later, she passed away. Before this talk, I had no idea the extent of Jesse's suffering or the resentment he harbored.

I was surprised to hear Jesse say I was his inspiration. He'd taken a DNA test but found it hard to understand. I encouraged him to stay positive and said I'd help.

"Jesse, don't lose hope. I've been on a quest for so long that I know the ropes by now. We can investigate legal records Jewish Services in New York City holds. Ancestry can turn up leads about your roots. I can guide you through the process. When you're ready to take the next step, let me know. We'll do it together."

"Oh, I'm ready. I might have siblings – not that you aren't enough – but, you get it, I know you do; they could be looking for me."

The Blue Ridge Parkway was the prettiest part of our trip. As we passed into South Carolina, I-95 ended, and so did my GPS guidance. Highway 521 took us straight into Georgetown.

Historic Georgetown is a quaint little town. Founded in 1729, it's South Carolina's third-oldest city, surrounded by rivers and steeped in history and charm. The streets downtown are lined with historic homes surrounded by sprawling live oak trees, Spanish moss dangling like tinsel from their ancient limbs. There's a thriving waterfront of restaurants, coffee shops, galleries and boutiques – all in refurbished buildings from a bygone era of mules and rice and dirt roads and sailing ships.

Credit goes to my cousin Eric for finding Pawleys Island;

after all he was there first. In any case, that was my destination. When we crossed the bridges that soar over the expansive waters of Winyah Bay they were shining as slick as glass and reflecting the setting sun; fifteen miles to go before Pawleys Island. We made it in time to check in our hotel and freshen up before heading to dinner where we savored hushpuppies, fresh shrimp, crab cakes and coleslaw.

The next day when I moved into my new apartment, Eric and his Pawleys' neighbors were there to help Jesse with the heavy stuff while I unloaded boxes and gave directions. At lunch one of the neighbors disappeared, returning with cooler laden with homemade pimiento cheese, chicken and shrimp salad sandwiches, chips, gallon jugs of iced tea, and a cooler full of ice. We ate outside on picnic tables on a beautiful May day and I started my new life in Pawleys surrounded by family and new friends.

# Chapter 43
## *Pawleys Island New Beginnings*

On Pawleys Island I found calm in the ever-changing tides of the Atlantic. I acclimated to the community, spent time with my cousin Eric and his son, invested in a good camera and grew into the habit of leaving the house in early morning darkness to catch the first glimmer of sunrise from the beach.

I found a job as a long-term substitute teacher at a middle school in Georgetown where I met Jacqueline, a Pennsylvania transplant. We became close, and talked about everything under the sun. When I mentioned my book project, she helped me with computer writing programs. By September, I was immersed in school life and had a routine. I was no longer part of the corporate rat race; teaching, photography, and writing were my new focus.

At the end of November I sent Dermod my new information and current research and he resumed sending me articles.

### Subject: Watch CBC documentary

*Diana! Glad to hear from you. You should watch, "I Think You've Been Looking for Me."*[18] *A reunion between a mother and son shows the misery caused by forced adoption and the ability of family to triumph. – Dermod*

The tranquility of settling in and enjoying my first winter on Pawleys was interrupted when a test found a tumor surrounding my thyroid. By the time I went for my recommended follow-up, its size had quadrupled. Fortunately only one gland out of four had to be removed. I felt blessed; and my new lease on life filled me with renewed determination to finish what I had started so long ago. Call it destiny or whatever you want, but the very day after my operation, I had an Ancestry email about a new, highly shared DNA match on my maternal side. I sent a message – with my phone number – to "Mario A.," and he called the next day.

He sounded a little bit nervous … and a little bit curious – and I felt the same. He said he was Darlene's son – (I know it's a lot to keep up with; Darlene was the baby sister of the Pauldino brothers, Michael and Daniel). Given our match, that made her my aunt! Mario and I now wondered – together – which of the brothers was my father.

I sent an email of thanks for his call and acknowledging the shock he must feel. I knew he needed time to process this news. In the meantime, I let him know I appreciated any pictures or details he might share – and I shared my own.

Mario hadn't spoken to Cheryl in at least twenty years, but knew enough to share her married name: Harrison. Thinking Luca might be interested in this new link, I sent him an email, only to be sorely disappointed when he replied:

### Subject: Aunt Darlene

*Diana,*
*I am sure you are a nice person … I have wonderful memories of my dad. I keep a small circle and am not looking to add anyone to my family. I will share photos with you. However, I won't test my DNA.*
*Luca*

I couldn't believe it. I cried all through the night. By morning I managed to pull myself together. Luca did share pictures of his dad and family, none of whom looked like me.

In the meantime I monitored Jesse's Ancestry account. In June, 2019, there was a hit from a DNA match that led to solving the mystery of his biological mother. When I finally made phone contact, I could hear the skeptical tone in her voice and let her process the shock. Having endured years of the pain of family secrets, I empathized. When we finally moved past that stage and began exchanging photos, we were both astonished by the unmistakable family resemblances, and Rosemary opened up.

"Diana, Mom never told my brother or me about a baby – much less one given up for adoption at six months! She would have been a month shy of her sixteenth birthday at the time; in those days, this kind of thing was never discussed."

DNA confirmed that Rosemary was Jesse's kid sister. On July 11, 2019, Jesse and Rosemary had a fantastic reunion. She didn't want to leave his side. Jesse was ecstatic. Rosemary hosted a huge barbecue in August, and Jesse and his girls were invited to meet their newfound family! My brother and nieces felt – and still feel – so blessed.

On the other hand, his brother was aloof about learning anything or having a relationship. People can't be forced. I advised Jesse to let it go and move forward.

Every once in a while, I heard from Dermod Travis. The last email I received from him was in the winter of 2020:

### Subject: Overseas Cold War

*Diana,*
*I believe you will find this email interesting. It features an article from the Toronto Star/The Canadian Press.*[19]

*Study reveals new details of Canadians' overseas Cold War intelligence effort.—a shadowy element of a little-known government program detailed in a newly declassified history.*

*Your mom was a fascinating woman with many secrets. The RCMP witness protection program didn't exist until 1970. Your mother's disappearance occurred in May 1967. With this in mind, remember they always protect their own. Your mom spent the 1960s in England, Switzerland, France, Germany, Austria, Poland, Hungary, Romania, Bulgaria, Ireland, and Cuba. She spoke five languages and was spotted alone in those countries – rather odd for the time. As you know, without proof of your being Donna's daughter, they'll tell you nothing. I trust you have your suspicions and can piece this together.*

*Dermod Travis*
*info@integritybc.ca*

Could Dermod be insinuating my mother was a spy?

# Chapter 44
## *I Will Survive!*

New Year's Day 2020: I followed my nose to the aroma of fresh coffee, poured myself a cup and set off to write. My goal for 2020 was to discover the missing pieces to my life's puzzle and finish my book.

Jesse jokingly replied he hoped to wake up every day. Then asked what Southerners ate on New Year's Day.

I listed black-eyed peas, pork, greens, and cornbread. Jesse made a face; none of these foods were our favorites – so I suggested we order Chinese. And we had a delightfully light-hearted New Year's Day – complete with chopsticks.

After the holidays I went back to work full-time. On the morning of March 13, 2020, I was on my way to school when I received a message that my services were no longer need-ed; COVID-19 had been declared a pandemic. By Monday school closures had impacted more than half of the coun-try; by month's end all public schools in the US were closed. Come May, the world had plunged into complete chaos. I couldn't write. I spent hours glued to the TV, shocked at the number of people dying all over the world. Sadness reigned. Quarantines were instituted. When we dared to go out, we donned masks and gloves, constantly used hand sanitizer, and maintained distance from others. It was a dreadful new norm.

By June, I had to do something, anything ... so I enrolled

in an online course and earned my teaching certification so I could tutor by Zoom. Still, I felt alone. I talked to God more, asking for strength, asking for courage.

It seemed like all news was bad news. Dermod Travis died in a hospital on the morning of June 1, 2020. I didn't even know he was ill. My tears wouldn't stop as I read about how he had sacrificed himself for others through-out his entire life.[20] I didn't know Der-mod personally, but he always believed in me and was always willing to help in my search for the truth.

Photo courtesy of Dermod Travis's sister Deirdre Chettleburgh

After Dermod passed, I fell into a deep funk. In all the years of life's ups and downs, I'd managed to stay positive. But this hit me hard. My photography friends on Facebook saved me. Over the next year our bond grew stronger. We brainstormed new ideas to keep our community engaged. The group sustained me through COVID and the turmoil that ensued – and it wasn't simply photography; it was about the connections we built and the support we provided.

I immersed myself in photography, tutoring, exploring my paternal ancestry, participating in art shows – and writing. In the end, I decided to streamline my schedule by prioritizing writing.

As if I needed to add to my isolation fatigue, I was diagnosed with vertigo – and my scoliosis worsened – but I refused to slow down. For the next five months, I was in physical therapy three times a week but I never stopped working on my manuscript.

I connected with Lily's daughter, Lindsay Low. Lindsay shared the heartbreaking news that her mom had passed away in March 2020. I offered my condolences: "Lily's warmth and persistence reflected her love for connecting with others and sharing her ideas, leaving an indelible mark on everyone she met."

It's remarkable how meaningful connections can form across distances. Though she's gone, I'm deeply grateful for the bond I shared with Lily. Her kindness, curiosity, and joy for life continue to inspire me, and I like to imagine she's smiling down, proud of the memories and connections she helped create.

I began engaging with the adoption community through Zoom calls and conferences. It all started with Adoption Happy Hour. Then I joined several other adoption groups and have built many wonderful connections. These groups are more than just a place to meet others – they're a source of support, understanding, and belonging. Through these connections, I've found people who truly understand my journey, shared stories that resonate deeply, and created bonds that continue to uplift and inspire me.

As my August birthday approached, my friends planned a luncheon for me – our first gathering in over a year. To their great surprise and happiness, I walked into the restaurant upright and unassisted. When it was time for champagne I stood tall, raised my glass, and toasted – "Nothing can stop me now!"

# Chapter 45
## *Inhale … Exhale*

Funny how I once thought writing the ending to this book would be easier than the beginning. But I'm still untangling details as I compose this final chapter.

My story would appear to have a life all its own …

I always post a photo and a few words about Mom on her birthday. In 2021, Donna Kolosky, born October 8, 1937, would have been 84 years old. My post had been up mere moments when I received a message informing me that Luca and Sofia's mother had passed. Today – October 8, 2021 – was the day of her funeral. The next day, I sent Luca a sympathy card.

On October 20th, I decided to write to my cousin, Mario A. one more time:

### Subject: Family Information

*Dear Mario,*
*I hope this message finds you and yours well. As I finalize my book, my focus is accuracy. With this in mind I seek your assistance locating a photograph of our Uncle Danny.*
*I recently learned Michael moved to Vancouver after his military service. I've managed to acquire his draft card, but have no more details. It is my sincere wish to honor your mother's beauty*

*and elegance in my book. Could you please share a brief para-graph or two about her? You'll be credited as the source.*
  *Warm wishes,*
  *Diana*

### Subject: Re: Michael and my mom

*Diana,*
*We are well, thank you. I hope you and yours are, too.*
*One correction: Uncle Michael never served in the military; Uncle Danny saw heavy combat during service in the Navy. I will try to come up with a few points about my mom.*
  *Regards,*
  *Mario*

Mario emailed a photo of Danny.

### Subject : Photo of Uncle Danny

*Dear Mario,*
*I have never seen a photo of Danny until today.*
*I know we've discussed Cheryl before, but I need to ask again … I'm desperate for more information – there's a good chance she could be my half-sister. A search through my Ancestry tree left me empty-handed. Any help from you is appreciated.*
  *Warm wishes, Diana*

Later, I created a photo of a side-by-side picture of Danny and me.

Mario wrote that evening.

### Subject: Info on Cheryl (Pauldino) Craciun Harrison etc.

*Diana,*
*Danny married Debbie (aka Elizabeth Mann), in 1957 in*

*Pueblo, Colorado. They then moved to Las Vegas where Cheryl was born on December 7, 1958. Prior to Debbie, Danny had been married once before.*

*In the 1950s, Debbie made her mark as a cocktail waitress in Vegas, while Danny worked as a blackjack dealer. After Debbie and Danny divorced, she married Joe Craciun and he legally adopted Cheryl. Cheryl took on her stepfather's surname – Craciun, and dropped her previous last name, Pauldino. If Debbie and Joe are still alive, I believe they remain married.*

*Cheryl was raised in Las Vegas, where she now lives with her husband, Ted Harrison. Cheryl took Ted's surname; she is active on Twitter.*

*I hope this helps.*
*Mario*

### Subject: Family ties and moving on

*Hi Mario,*
*If Danny is my father, then Cheryl is my half-sibling.*
*Though I am grateful for my incredible adoptive father and would never want to replace him, I feel a connection to my biological father.*
*I understand it's not unusual for families to keep secrets, but I feel the time has come for me to move on, put this matter to rest, and focus on the rest of my life's journey.*
*Warm wishes,*
*Diana*

I took a chance and wrote Cheryl Harrison at an address I found online. I kept things light, telling her about Grandmother Ruby and my first cousin Mario. I included my email address, phone number, and a picture.

I joined Jesse on a drive to Florida to visit Rosemary and old friends in Sarasota; I mailed the letter to Cheryl on the way. It was October 29.

In Sarasota my long-time friend Stacey and I caught up over lunch downtown. When she asked how my book was coming along, I was thrilled to tell her I was writing the final chapters. Her eyes lit up with enthusiasm. She'd been involved since my story began the spring of 1993. It seemed like only yesterday. Before we knew it, our time was up. As was our routine when we parted, we hugged, saying 'See you soon,' rather than 'goodbye.'

Home in Pawleys a week later, I checked the mail, my hopes dimming when I saw nothing from Cheryl.

Jesse said, "Relax, you only mailed the letter last week. Put yourself in her shoes; news like that takes some processing; give her some time."

Of course he was right. I went about my daily routine and kept busy with photography. I was having a coffee break and idly flipping through my phone when I saw a missed voicemail from a Las Vegas number.

I inhaled, prepared for the worst.

"Hello, this is Cheryl Harrison. I have just received your letter and would appreciate it if you could call me back."

Oh my oh my ... this call could be a making or breaking point. I was nervous so I called Steve for a pep rally. As always, he had my back and bolstered my confidence.

"Just be yourself. You've come so far! I believe Cheryl will support you – and if she doesn't, we'll handle that, too."

So I called, introduced myself, and tried to nutshell my tale ... my birth in Canada, being sold as a black market baby, the unexpected revelation of my adoption, the trips to Canada and Colorado, the DNA tests, my relationship with the Pauldino family ... and though she sounded apprehensive at first, once Cheryl realized the scope of my search, I heard comfort replace caution in her voice. We talked for hours.

Cheryl confirmed all Mario said. She was born in Las Vegas in 1958 where her parents were married; they divorced in '62 when she was four. Her mom Debbie remarried. Joseph and Debbie Craciun currently live in Vegas. Joseph is five years younger than Debbie and has been a craps dealer for fifty-nine years. The Pauldino name vanished when Joe Craciun adopted her.

I exhaled; this gal was the real thing.

As the conversation progressed Cheryl talked about Danny and Michael's mob connections in Vegas AND in Denver, specifically with the Smaldones and the Rat Pack. It seems he had a phenomenal memory for numbers and was regarded as a math whiz. I couldn't help but mention I was a math teacher.

Cheryl recalled getting dressed in her Sunday best to visit Uncle Mike in the Federal Penitentiary in Leavenworth, Kansas.

The only thing Cheryl's mother had known about Danny's life before her was he had been married once before. Cheryl's father, Danny, was a blackjack dealer in Las Vegas and taught snow skiing part-time at Lee Canyon, just outside the city.

Wait. What? I interrupted. "Danny was the ski instructor, not Michael?"

"That's right. Michael never skied."

"AND … Michael served another prison term for refusing to inform. I read *Smaldone: The Untold Story of an American Crime Family* by Dick Kreck. In the book, Michael Pauldino discusses a gunfight that occurred at an ice cream parlor he owned. According to Mafia tradition, if someone is convicted of a crime they didn't commit, they're expected to serve the sentence rather than participate with the police. In Mafia culture, violation is punishable by death."

Cheryl recalled reading testimony from an FBI agent about an incident in 1966 that quoted Michael Pauldino describing himself as a professional gambler.

"What about Debbie? Can you tell me more about your mother?"

"Mom grew up in an orphanage and was adopted by the Mann family from Pennsylvania and became Elizabeth Mann. As soon as she could she left the east coast for Denver and changed her name to Debbie.

"I married my husband, Ted Harrison, in 1992. Ted is originally from Vancouver, British Columbia; he became a United States citizen in 1989. Eight years into our marriage, we adopted two children."

That sentence was my cue; I asked if she would consider doing a DNA test, offering to buy the kit as a gift. A few days later, Cheryl agreed to a test.

"Ultimately, my father lived in Denver with his sister, Darlene. He was broke and unwell and died from COPD and emphysema on December 13, 1995."

The more we talked, the more I felt her warming to the idea that Danny might well be my father – and she, my half-sister! I sent a few photos, hoping she might see the family resemblance.

Ten days later, she informed me she had received her DNA kit. I told her I would answer any questions about the test and the results; after all, this was old hat to me. While we waited for results she promised to look for photos.

As I thought about Cheryl's DNA test, I remembered my surprise at how complicated understanding the results was when I took my first test. Every name on the result list represented a DNA secret, introducing me to relatives who were, up to that point, strangers.

As time passed, I reached out to new cousins and found many supportive relatives. In the spring of 2019, Mario A. was identified as my paternal first cousin. He was the breakthrough in my DNA research that eventually led me to Cheryl Harrison. I sent Mario an email.

**Subject: Update on Cheryl**

*Hello, Mario,*

*Thanks to you, Cheryl and I have finally connected! I'm thrilled that she has agreed to take a DNA test. We're excitedly awaiting the results.*

*During our conversation, I mentioned you; she said it's been a while but would look forward to catching up with you. Here's her number: xxx-xxx-xxxx. I'm eager to see how everything unfolds!*

*Take care,*

*Diana*

On Thanksgiving, Cheryl and I exchanged text messages – an act I hoped would become tradition. I must say I was quite beside myself at the thought of a new family member.

Cheryl's response was heartwarming: "We are hosting a small gathering and thinking of you. Hope your day is filled with love and happiness. Let's make plans to catch up soon."

Through this simple exchange I could feel how special our bond was, reinforcing ways DNA testing uncovers truths and changes the makeup of families.

Cheryl's DNA results were still not back. Our conversations settled into a routine; we shared snippets of our lives as I put the finishing touches on my book. Her stories and memories were timed perfectly to enliven the narrative and she continued to remember stories about Michael:

"Aside from our prison visits I only saw Uncle Mike a handful of times. I thought it was funny how he talked out of the side of his mouth, just like the gangsters did in *The Godfather*."

"Did he stuff his cheeks with Kleenex like Marlon Brando did in *The Godfather* movies?"

Laughing at the memory, Cheryl replied, "When he was in prison, he was private chef for the warden. I don't think he was much of a cook before that."

"That sounds like a scene straight out of *Goodfellas*. I can picture him eating lobster, drinking wine, and smoking Cubans with the warden."

Cheryl's stories painted a picture of a family struggling to function normally in the face of addiction and crime. "Danny took me shopping for school clothes every year and taught me how to ski when I was nine, but the consequences of his addiction ended up keeping us apart until my thirties. Sister Darlene held the family together. She took care of the aunties – as well as Michael and Danny – emotionally, physically, and financially – sometimes at the expense of her marriage."

The wait for the DNA results became a period of reflection for us. It felt like we were weaving together the fragmented pieces of our past.

On the drive to Florida for Christmas I spoke with my Uncle Kenny for the first time. We had been in contact on social media for months; he was a son of Grandmother Ruby Wilkerson Pauldino. He was eighty-three. I hoped to get to know him better in the upcoming New Year.

I divided my holiday time between family and friends. Though I stayed with my friends Catalina and Victor at their dreamy house on Treasure Island, my son and his wife had recently celebrated their tenth wedding anniversary in Italy and bought a new home in Tampa where we all gathered for a delightful Christmas Eve. It was wonderful to reconnect with David and his bride. Everyone who knows me at all knows I consider my son to be my greatest gift; he has become a man to be quite proud of.

I vowed to my Florida friends and family that I'd keep working on the final chapter of my book and submit the completed manuscript. Catalina had expressed a keen interest and insisted on reading a chapter. Her enthusiasm fueled my motivation to wrap things up.

Victor's brother-in-law Luis was visiting from Miami. A native of Cuba, Victor had told Luis about my story; Luis was especially interested in Mom's trip to Cuba in August 1959. I showed him footage from the Kodachrome slides and the photos. Amazingly, Luis recognized everyone except for the Mystery Man in trunks. He not only recognized them but also knew their backgrounds. I spent the rest of the night mesmerized by tales of Cuba.

"From left to right are Raul Castro, Fidel Castro, and the unknown man in the middle. In the film, I see Ramon Castro and Juan Almeida Bosque. Raul was the last to join. Look closely: Ramon pulls a book from his right hand, opens it, and reads it aloud."

(L to R) Raul Castro, Fidel Castro, unidentified, Fidel Castro, unidentified (Errol Flynn? CIA?), Juan Almeida Bosque, Ramon Castro.

"Luis, I apologize for the blurry photos but I believe they contribute to my story."

"Oh, the film is clear enough. The more I look and think of the time, the more I assume the man in the trunks is CIA. I recommend you read *Bohemia Cuba Magazine*, the Bohemia Vintage 1959 edition. I will email you the information."[21]

Thanks to Luis I learned for the first time that Juan Almeida Bosque was on the other side of the Mystery Man. Luis's knowledge of Cuba filled in some blanks of my mom's time in Cuba.

I thanked Catalina, Victor, and Luis for a Christmas I'll never forget.

By January 5, 2023, Cheryl's DNA results confirmed she was my first cousin – not my half-sister. As disappointing as this discovery was, it revealed a complex history with Danny and Michael – whom I now knew were Uncle Danny and my dad, Michael. When I mulled it over, I imagined Michael's fascinating stories from Leavenworth and being on the FBI's most-wanted list. And I spent the next five months researching.

Michael was a lifetime member of the Smaldone organized crime family. Nicknamed 'Mikie,' spent time in Seattle, Vancouver, Las Vegas, and Denver – his hometown.

An online search turned up a book on Amazon, *Pauldino (Michael E.) v. U.S. U.S. Supreme Court Transcript of Record with Supporting Pleadings by Dennis L. Blewitt and Erwin N. Griswold.*[22] I decided to do more research.

Erwin N. Griswold argued many cases before the U.S. Supreme Court, served as the Solicitor General of the United States, and Dean of Harvard Law School. On several occasions, he was considered to serve on the U.S. Supreme Court.

Dennis L. Blewitt lives in Loveland, Colorado as a semi-retired lawyer. After reaching out to Dennis on Facebook, we became friends and have spoken by phone several times. He was my father's lawyer and practiced criminal defense and securities law for decades. He currently consults, writes, and maintains a political blog. In our talks he described Michael as "distinguished, charming, and likable ..."

An anonymous source revealed Michael and a gambler friend worked for Jack Ruby during the late 1950s smuggling guns and ammunition in caskets from Texas to Cuba. On the way back, they used armored cars to smuggle heroin and guns through Mexico in what the source claimed was a government operation.

During one of my first conversations with Cheryl she told me she spent her middle school summers visiting her father, Aunt Darlene, and cousin Mario in Denver, explaining, "It was June. We were visiting Uncle Mike at Leavenworth as a family. We dressed in our Sunday best, with Aunt Darlene showing off her mink – in JUNE, mind you! We got used to seeing barbed-wire gates and armed officers in the tower."

Still, it must have caused Cheryl some emotional pain – seeing Uncle Mike in prison even if his crime ties landed him a cushy job as the warden's private chef.

The newfound knowledge brought back childhood memories … I guess I was lucky to have been at camp while Cheryl was stuck visiting a prison.

I've read stories about happy reunions, joyful moments when one meets their biological mother, father, or both. Looking back, knowing my mother's identity should have been enough closure. But it wasn't; I wanted more.

It took me seven years after taking a DNA test to find my biological father. For years I thought he was Canadian. Truth was, he was Michael Eugene Pauldino, born October 26, 1926, died July 27, 2015. His parents were Ruby and Danny Pauldino Sr.; their parents – my great-grandparents – were Michael Pauldino Sr. and Antonette Route from Potenza, Basilicata, Italy.

Danny Pauldino        Diana Hochberg        Michael Pauldino

Over time I have found my half-brother and -sister, children from later years of Michael's life, Luca and Sofia. I will never have a relationship with them – and that's okay. They both loved their dad, and he was a good father to them.

So. After all of these years of searching for my father, Michael seems more like a character straight out of a movie than a real guy.

Apparently, I have another book to write. I'll need another lifetime.

# EPILOGUE

What began so simply – a casual remark over lunch in Las Vegas – spiraled into a journey that would change my life forever. Twenty-nine years of doubt, disappointment, and relentless research led me through a labyrinth of secrets: the black-market baby trade, corrupt government systems, the Mafia, and even the CIA. Every thread I pulled unraveled a deeper web of power, money, and deception. I came to understand that corruption wasn't an anomaly – it was the cost of doing business, accepted by every political party and high-ranking official.

But along the way, I found truth. I found strength. And I found myself.

Thanks to people like Dermod Travis, James Hourston, and countless others – friends, family, and even strangers who believed in me – I uncovered not just answers, but stories of courage and resilience. Their unwavering support and my own resolve turned my search into something greater than I could have imagined. I became stronger, more informed, and part of a global community of truth-seekers who refuse to give up.

My passion for genealogy became my compass. Using Ancestry, I traced my lineage back to the Revolutionary War, uncovering ties to the Ashby family in Fauquier, Virginia, and the Hardins of Charleston, South Carolina. These discoveries led me to apply to the Winyah Chapter of the Daughters of the American Revolution and reconnect with newfound cousins. Each piece of my family's history felt like reclaiming a part of myself.

Yet, obstacles remain. Under Canadian law, my mother's citizenship should extend to me, but without documentation, I remain in limbo. Proving I am Donna's daughter is an uphill battle, complicated by the absence of her DNA and the silence of her siblings. As I fought to reclaim my identity, I also uncovered the complex and mysterious life of my mother, Donna Kole.

Her death in 1967 is shrouded in ambiguity, with stories ranging from tragedy to survival. Dr. Claude Hardwick claimed to have saved her life, recalling her whispered plea: "Save me." Donna's family believes she died that year, yet the evidence I've gathered suggests three possibilities: she could still be alive, living in Europe under a pseudonym, or residing in Langley under an entirely new identity. I may never know the full truth.

Nearly every morning, I take my camera to the wide, white beaches of Pawleys Island. The roar of the waves and the scent of the ocean transport me to a place of reflection and peace. I plant my chair in the sand, dig my toes into the earth, and watch the sunrise. Thin bands of light explode into a kaleidoscope of color, filling the sky with possibility. It's here, on the cusp of a new day, that I feel closest to Donna, the mother I never knew.

Some mornings, as I sit there, I imagine I'm in Vancouver, standing outside the Sylvia Hotel. A woman walks along the seawall with a Havanese on a leash. She's wearing a red belted trench coat, a gold designer watch, a silk scarf, and aviators. It's her – Donna. I imagine her watching me all these years, knowing me better than anyone else could. After all, she is my mother. She hated being poor, and perhaps, in her way, she ensured I'd live the life she couldn't.

Mort once told me about the night we crossed the border, just three weeks after I was born. Donna made the impossible choice to give me up, ensuring I'd be loved and protected. That choice saved us both, even as it broke her heart. As I reflect on her sacrifice, I feel an overwhelming sense of gratitude, even in the face of unanswered questions.

Today, as I leave the beach and step into the next chapter of my life, I carry with me a new understanding. This journey has given me answers, but more importantly, it has given me peace. I've learned that love transcends time, separation, and even death.

To those who are searching for their own truth, I hope my story reminds you that the pursuit of answers is worth every step, no matter how painful or uncertain the path may be. The mysteries we uncover shape us, but they don't define us. What matters most is the love we carry and the strength we find along the way. I hope my journey inspires you to seek your own truths, to embrace the struggles and triumphs along the way, and to trust that even the most difficult paths can lead to peace and understanding.

As the tide pulls back and the horizon stretches before me, I whisper, "Thank you, Mom." And for the first time, I feel her answer – in the waves, the wind, and the sunlight on my face.

# END NOTES

**Chapter 19**

[1]Lawrence, Grant. "Seventy sinful years of the Penthouse Nightclub." Vancouver is Awesome. https://www.vancouverisawesome.com/courier-archive/news/seventy-sinful-years-of-the-penthouse-nightclub-3062364. November 20, 2017.

**Chapter 20**

[2]"VanDusen Botanical Gardens." City of Vancouver Guides. https://vancouver.ca/parks-recreation-culture/vandusen-botanical-garden.aspx. February 2018.

**Chapter 26**

[3]Zerobyte. "Hotel Nacional de Cuba: A mix of history and Cuban Culture." Havanna Tour. https://www.vintagecarstours.com/hotel-nacional-de-cuba-a-mix-of-history-and-cuban-culture/. August 19, 2022.

[4]Editors of Encyclopaedia Britannica. "Cuban Revolution." *Encyclopedia Britannica*. https://www.britannica.com/event/Cuban-Revolution. January 21, 2024.

[5]Koo, Sheena. "The Incredible History of The Penthouse: A Vancouver Landmark Weathers 70 Years of Change." Vancouver Police Museum & Archives. https://www.vancouverpolicemuseum.ca/post/the-incredible-history-of-the-penthouse-a-vancouver-landmark-weathers-70-years-of-change. July 4, 2019.

[6]Moody, Erica. "Ybor City History." TAMPA.GOV. https://www.tampa.gov/CRAs/ybor-city/history. October 1, 2023.

**Chapter 28**

[7]Flores, Reena. "President Obama welcomed in Cuba on historic visit." CBS News. https://www.cbsnews.com/news/president-obama-welcomed-in-cuba-on-historic-visit/. March 20, 2016.

## Chapter 29

[8]Balcom, Karen. "Phony Mothers and Border-Crossing Adoptions: The Montreal-to-New York Black Market in Babies in the 1950s." *Journal of Women's History* 19(1):107-116. DOI: 10.1353/jowh.2007.0003. https://www.researchgate.net/publication/236816169_Phony_Mothers_and_Border-Crossing_Adoptions_The_Montreal-to-New_York_Black_Market_in_Babies_in_the_1950s. March 2007.

[9]Hamilton, Janice. "MONTREAL'S BLACK MARKET BABIES." Genealogy Ensemble. https://genealogyensemble.com/2014/04/04/montreals-black-market-babies/. April 4, 2014.

[10]"MK/Black Market Babies" Jewish Adoptions, 1930s – 1950s + Black Market Baby Scandal. MKUltra experimentation. Keep the Ethical Light Burning. https://keepkelb.com/f-black-market-babies-mkultra/. February 16, 2011.

## Chapter 31

[11]Timbrell, Don (Columbian Photo). "Joe Plaskett and Mrs. Jack Hardman admiring painting – 1962." New Westminster Archives. http://archives.newwestcity.ca/permalink/63673/. 1962.

## Chapter 35

[12]Mackie, Jack. "This Week in History, 1952: Jack Wasserman comes out After Dark." *Vancouver Sun.* https://vancouversun.com/news/local-news/this-week-in-history-1952-jack-wasserman-comes-out-after-dark. April 15, 2022.

[13]Lazarus, Eve. "Italian Heritage Month – meet the East End's Angelo Branca." Every Place Has a Story. https://evelazarus.com/italian-heritage-month-meet-the-east-ends-angelo-branca/. June 17, 2017.

## Chapter 38

[14]Hendry, Leah. "How one man's search for Quebec adoption records turned into a 'wild goose chase'." CBC News. https://www.cbc.ca/news/canada/montreal/how-one-man-s-search-for-quebec-adoption-records-turned-into-a-wild-goose-chase-1.4306144. September 27, 2017.

## Chapter 41

[15]Masich, Matt. "Smaldone, Denver's Mob." *Colorado Life Magazine.* Article by Matt Masich. https://www.coloradolifemagazine.com/print-page/post/index/id/128.

[16]Singer, Daliah. "Five Things You Didn't Know About Gaetano's." *5280-Mile-High Magazine*. https://www.5280.com/gaetanos-turns-70/. November 9, 2017.

**Chapter 42**

[17]Brennan, Noel. "Storytellers: Adoptees share secrets, search for family." *Denver News* 9. https://www.9news.com/article/news/local/story-tellers/storytellers-bringing-secrets-into-the-open/73-565196242. June 17, 2018.

**Chapter 43**

[18]Azouz, Dorothy Steets. "I Think You've Been Looking For Me." CBC documentary POV. www.cbc.ca/cbcdocspov/episodes/i-think-youve-been-looking-for-me. July 2018.

[19]Bronskill, Jim. "Study reveals new details of overseas Cold War intelligence effort by Canadians." The Canadian Press / *Toronto Star*. https://www.thestar.com/news/canada/study-reveals-new-details-of-overseas-cold-war-intelligence-effort-by-canadians/article_b5eab382-bf23-53b1-a5f2-e0ab1a54ff49.html. August 25, 2019.

**Chapter 44**

[20]"B.C. political watchdog Dermod Travis has died." Times Colonist staff / *Vancouver Sun*. https://vancouversun.com/news/b-c-political-watchdog-dermod-travis-has-died. June 2, 2020.

**Chapter 45**

[21]"Bohemia Cuba Magazine." Edition Bohemia Vintage 1959. https://www.cubacollectibles.com/cuba-B-59-02-01.html.

[22]Blewitt, Dennis L., and Erwin N. Griswold. "Pauldino (Michael E.) v. U.S. U.S. Supreme Court Transcript of Record with Supporting Pleadings." https://www.amazon.com/Pauldino-Michael-Transcript-Supporting-Pleadings/dp/1270579657. October 30, 2011.

# APPENDIX A
## Persons in *Connected* identified by their real names

Aaron Chapman: Prominent figure in Vancouver, known for his work as a writer, historian, and musician.

Abraham and Anna Hochberg (both deceased): My adopted aunt and uncle. Parents of Roberta Hochberg.

Alex Kreedman: The son of Richard and Michele Kreedman.

Althea McCartie (deceased): Rick's mother, who shares her knowledge of Vancouver and her late husband's connections.

Andrée (deceased): Mort Shulman's mistress.

Angelo Branca (deceased): BC Supreme Court Judge and Court of Appeals Judge, mentioned in the friend's text.

Ann Margret: Performer mentioned by Diana in Las Vegas.

Anne Diamond (deceased): Manny Diamond's wife.

Anne May (deceased): A friend of Gabriel and Sylvia, who shares stories of her late husband, a jazz musician.

Annie Bilyk Kolosky/Koloski (deceased): Annie, was my maternal biological grandmother, she spent over thirty-five years as a waitress at the Aristocrat Restaurant in Vancouver, remembered for her strong work ethic and resilience.

Annie Cohen: Buyer/Marketing/Public Relations for Browns Shoes. A person Diana contacts for help regarding her mother's photo and connection to Browns Shoes.

Antonette Route (deceased): Diana's great-grandmother on her biological paternal side. Her lineage and life play a significant role in understanding the family's history and heritage.

Aunt Dot/Dorothy Koloski (deceased): My biological maternal aunt, was a talented watercolor artist living in Langley with her long-time roommate, Marty Holmes. She exudes elegance and shares valuable family history, helping me connect with my mother, Donna.

Aunt Jan/Janet Kolosky/Koloski/Henriksen /McConnell (deceased): Biological maternal aunt from North Burnaby, BC. A practical individual, Jan is dedicated to preserving family history. Despite her care, she often lies and keeps secrets, playing an antagonistic role in revealing family mysteries and dealing with Diana's quest for truth.

Aunt Rebecca Hochberg (deceased): Diana's adoptive aunt.

B. Lapointe: A representative of the Ministerial Enquiries Division who responds to Diana's letter to the Prime Minister, providing information on how to apply for Canadian citizenship confirmation.

Barry Dykes: An archivist in New Westminster, BC, who assists Diana with her family history research.

Barry Peacock (deceased): A Montreal native living in Vancouver for over twenty-three years who takes Diana on a nostalgic tour of Vancouver and offers assistance in her research.

Basil Pantage (deceased): Mentioned in the friend's text as a stock promoter, nightclub owner, and president of the annual Polar Bear swim in Vancouver.

Beatrice: Spoke with Port Moody Fire Rescue.

Bebop: Gabriel and Sylvia's dog, a Shih Tzu and Schnauzer mix.

Ben Weider (deceased): Joe Weider's brother, also influential in the bodybuilding community.

Billy Cox: He is a reporter from Sarasota who has encouraged Diana in her pursuits.

Bon Jovi: Mentioned in conversation about his concert in Vancouver.

Bonnie Garramone (deceased): An eighty-six-year-old genealogy expert, is a vibrant and dedicated figure in the Italian community of Denver, known for her extensive contributions to family history research. She mentors Diana, offering valuable advice and encouragement as they explore their shared heritage.

Brent Corbie: Close friend and invites her to stay at his house.

British Columbia Vital Statistics: The institution that provided Diana with a death certificate containing incorrect information about her mother.

Carlo Gallo (deceased): A man linked to the Vancouver Mafia.

Carlos Olivera: A highly skilled makeup artist and Diana's colleague who suggests contacting Cristina Puig.

Carol Chycoski: Carol Chycoski, a friend from Vancouver, played a key role in providing information about Doris Langerak and her mother.

CBC Investigates: The division of the CBC mentioned in relation to Ken Waisanen's story about searching for Quebec adoption records.

Cheryl Pauldino Harrison: A pivotal figure in Diana's quest to uncover her family history. Cheryl is initially believed to be a potential half-sister but is later confirmed through DNA testing to be Diana's paternal first cousin.

Chris D'Orlando: Diana's ex-coworker from Florida who lives near Denver and spends weekends exploring with her.

Claire Marie Whiteman: She is the stepdaughter of the author Diana Kayla Hochberg from a previous marriage of Diana's late husband, Stephen.

Colleen Shannon Fisher: Diana's biological paternal cousin who connected Diana with Lisa Shannon through social media. Colleen lives in Arizona but is originally from Denver.

Cristina Puig: A news anchor in Tampa who Diana reaches out to for assistance.

D. Armstrong: Executive Correspondence Officer who responds to Diana's letter to Prime Minister Justin Trudeau, explaining that the Prime Minister cannot personally intervene in her situation.

Daniel Pauldino Jr. (deceased): Another son of Ruby's and a potential candidate for Diana's biological father.

Daniel Pauldino, Sr. (deceased): Ruby's first husband and Diana's paternal grandfather, whose lineage connects to the Route family.

Danny Filippone: The current owner of the Penthouse Nightclub in Vancouver, a historic venue renowned for its colorful past and significant cultural impact.

Daphne Bramham: A journalist who Dermod suggests might interview Diana about her story. She is in Regina with her mother in the hospital and communicates with Diana via email.

David Hochberg: Diana's son, who accompanies her on her journey to uncover her true identity and meets their Canadian family.

David Quint: A filmmaker and friend of Diana's who she meets for lunch in Denver.

David Thaler: Joanne's twin son, also referred to as "mom's favorite twin son." Bio Paternal cousin.

Deirdre Chettleburgh: Photo courtesy of Dermon Travis's sister, who lives in Victoria, British Columbia, Canada.

Dennis L. Blewitt (deceased): Michael Pauldino's lawyer for over twenty-five years.

Dermod Travis (deceased): A man with many affiliations, including Integrity BC, who assists Diana in uncovering details about her mother's history and other related investigations.

Diana Kayla Hochberg: The protagonist, who embarks on a quest to uncover her true identity after discovering she was adopted.

Donna Koloski / Donna Cole, Kole, and Camilla Marilyn Kolosky (deceased): Diana's biological mother born as Camilla Marilyn Koloski on October 8, 1937, and later renamed Donna by her family, she was a vibrant, multilingual woman known for her love of dogs, outdoor sports, and high fashion. She moved to Montreal and graduated from McGill University in 1959.

Doris Langerak (deceased): Mutual friend of Donna, Dot, and Jan.

Dr. Jason C. Rosenberg, MD: A South Carolina physician who writes the foreword for Diana's story.

Dustin Overmyer (deceased): Stephanie's late brother, identified as Diana's second cousin on the biological paternal side.

Ed Cosgrove (deceased): The photojournalist who took the first bikini photo of Donna.

Ed Neues: Ilene's husband and friend to Diana. Live in Denver, Co.

Elizabeth and Martin Meier: Owners of The Goddard School where Diana applies for a job.

Elizabeth Mann/Debbie: Cheryl's mother and Danny's ex-wife, a former cocktail waitress at a Vegas casino.

Elvis Presley (deceased): Mentioned in a story by Mr. Manny Hochberg.

ER Doctor: Provides advice to Diana in the emergency room.

Eric Teague: A paternal cousin of Diana's, who contacts her through Ancestry and shares many similarities with her. He helps Diana uncover more about their shared family history.

Erica Heuer-Hochberg: Diana's daughter-in-law, married to her son David Hochberg.

Errol Flynn (deceased): Mentioned as a historical figure who visited the Penthouse Nightclub before his death.

Erwin N. Griswold (deceased): Appellate attorney involved in Michael Pauldino case.

Ethan Baron: Business reporter for the *Mercury News* in Silicon Valley, California.

Ethel Hochberg (née Eres, deceased): Diana's adoptive mother, who passed away before Diana's eleventh birthday

Eve Abrams: A woman from Honolulu, now living in Vancouver, who befriends Diana at the Comedy Club.

Evelyn Johnstone (deceased): Rod Hourston's late wife.

Fidel Castro (deceased): Cuban leader, potentially appearing in the films.

Fran Route (deceased): A non-blood relative who welcomes Diana to her home and introduces her to other family members in Denver, Colorado.

Francine: A woman from Vancouver who meets Diana at Lonsdale Quay and shares information about her past and clairvoyant abilities.

Frank/Fred Koloski-Kulchisky (deceased) He was my biological maternal grandfather. He was a gambler, known for his daring and adventurous spirit.

Gabriel Mark Hasselbach: He is my cousin on paternal side. A Canadian jazz musician known for his work as a trumpeter and flugelhornist.

Gerry DiSalvo (deceased): A man linked to the Vancouver Mafia.

Giuseppe/Joe Gentile and Gerry Di Salvo (deceased): Mentioned as owners of Casa d' Italia in Vancouver.

Gordon Clark: A reporter for *The Province* newspaper in Vancouver, BC, Canada.

Grace Edgin: Diana's friend and coworker who shared her foster care experience during a farewell brunch at Europa Coffeehouse. They promised to stay in touch despite Grace moving to Washington, D.C.

Harold Rosenberg: A black-market adoptee and former police photographer, who assists Diana by sharing his own experiences and knowledge.

Heather Hartmann: Greets Diana at The Goddard School.

Honourable Ahmed Hussen: Minister of Immigration, Refugees and

Citizenship who is supposed to have read the original letter sent by Diana to Prime Minister Trudeau but appears to have not read it.

Ilene Neues: Diana's childhood friend in Denver, who takes her out to lunch and rekindles old memories.

Jack Ruby (deceased): He was an American nightclub owner who gained notoriety for fatally shooting Lee Harvey Oswald, the alleged assassin of President John F. Kennedy, adding a layer of mystery to the Kennedy assassination conspiracy theories. Dennis mentioned that Michael and his friend worked for Jack in a smuggling operation during the 1950s.

Jack Wasserman (deceased): Nightlife and celebrity columnist for Vancouver.

James Dubro: Crime novelist, documentary TV producer, investigative journalist, and bookseller. Engages in extensive communication with Diana and meets her in Ybor City.

James Hourston (deceased): Diana's friend from Vancouver who assists her in researching her mother's past and navigating the city.

James Sanseverino/Jim or Jimmy San Severino (deceased): Joe Gentile's right-hand man.

James Van Velson: Another match in Diana's family research, cousin paternal side.

Janice Johnston: A genealogist and Diana's cousin on her maternal side, who helps her with DNA research.

Jeanne Balanik-Kolosky (deceased): My aunt through marriage to Uncle Ron. She lived on Vancouver Island.

Jesse Hochberg: Diana's adopted brother, who provides support and information as she uncovers her true identity.

Jim Millar: Manager and curator of the Port Moody Station Museum. Friend of Ed Cosgrove.

Joanne and Ron Thaler (deceased): Joanne is Gabriel's aunt and Diana's older cousin in Wheat Ridge, who welcomes her into their home and shares family stories.

Joe (Philliponi)/Fillippone/Filippone Jimmy, Ross, and Mickey Filippone (all deceased): Four brothers founded the Penthouse Nightclub in Vancouver.

Joe Craciun: Debbie's second husband and Cheryl's adoptive father.

Joe Klein (deceased): A person who wrote a heartfelt eleven-page love letter to Diana's father, revealing complex details about Diana's adoption and family secrets.

Joe Romano (deceased): A man linked to the Vancouver Mafia.

Joe Weider (deceased): Influential in the bodybuilding world, mentioned as a potential associate of significant figures in Montreal's history.

John Fuller: Reporter in Vancouver.

John Grasty: A real estate agent who helps Diana with information about her grandmother's property and connects her with Vince Chessa.

John Route: Fran's son and Diana's third cousin on my paternal side who helped connect Diana with Fran.

Joseph Francis Plaskett (deceased): Joseph Plaskett was an artist from New Westminster who had a connection to Diana's family through her grandmother, whom he met while she worked as a waitress. His paintings, especially of Arlington Apartments where her family lived, hold emotional value for Diana, linking her to her family's past in Vancouver.

Joseph Gentile (deceased): Also known as Giuseppe, was a powerful and enigmatic mob boss in Vancouver with deep ties to organized crime. He co-owned Casa D'Italia, a front for laundering money between Vancouver and Montreal. With a dark and mysterious aura, he adds a menacing and influential presence to the story.

Juan Almeida Bosque (deceased): He was identified by Victor in the film. Victor said Juan was a Cuban politician and one of the original commanders of the insurgent forces in the Cuban Revolution.

Justin Trudeau: The Prime Minister of Canada to whom Diana writes a letter seeking assistance in uncovering her mother's records and reclaiming her Canadian heritage.

Karen Balcom: Professor with a Ph.D. in Modern U.S. History and Women's History, author of *The Traffic in Babies*, who assists Diana with her research.

Karen Schwimmer: A fellow passenger on the flight to Denver who shares her own adoption story with Diana.

Kathy White-Fuller (deceased): A close friend and coworker of Diana from Clearwater, FL, originally from Hell's Kitchen, New York City. She supported Diana during her transition to Clearwater.

Ken Waisanen: An adoptee mentioned in an article forwarded by Dermod, who is trying to find his birth father and relevant medical history.

Kenneth Teague: Eric's great-uncle and Diana's half-uncle, as confirmed by a DNA test on paternal side.

Lady at Parker Street: Current resident of Diana's grandmother's house.

Lily Grouix (deceased): She was a friend of Donna and later became Diana's friend after a newspaper article connected them. They stayed in touch through letters and calls, with Lily supporting Diana in uncovering her family's past.

Lindsay Low: Lily's daughter, who informed Diana about her mother's passing in March 2020.

Lisa Shannon: Diana's biological paternal cousin living in Turkey for 14 years. They met at The French Press café, bonded over family history, and shared stories. Lisa is supportive of Diana's journey.

Lorenzo Dardano: A regular at Gaetano's Italian Restaurant who provides Diana with information about the Pauldino family and their connections to the Mafia.

Maître d': The maître d' at The Palm Court in the Plaza Hotel.

Maître d': A staff member at Hawksworth who interacts with James and the narrator during their lunch.

Manny Diamond (deceased): A close friend of Diana's adoptive father, Manny Hochberg, and the former CIA agent who reveals to Diana that she was adopted, initiating her journey to uncover her true identity.

Manny Hochberg (deceased): Diana's adoptive father who raised her, often referred to as her dad, father, and daddy.

Mark Enquist: A friend of Diana's with whom she shares mutual interests and chemistry. They meet for coffee and drinks, and Mark offers to help Diana with her investigation in Canada.

Marty/Marlene Holmes (deceased): Dot's roommate and life partner.

Mary (Marigold) Hardwick (deceased): Dr. Hardwick's wife, who assists in the conversation and provides additional insights.

Mary: Rosemary and Jesse's biological mother, who kept Jesse's adoption a secret.

Michael Pauldino (deceased): A man deeply involved with the Smaldone crime family, whose complex life story Diana uncovers. He was one of Ruby's sons and a potential candidate for Diana's biological father.

Michael Pauldino Sr., (deceased): Diana's great-grandfather, on her biological paternal side who hailed from Potenza, Basilicata, Italy.

Michele Kreedman: Diana's best friend, who, along with her husband Richard, invites Diana and her son David to join them in Las Vegas to support Diana after her husband's sudden death

Mickey Mantle (deceased): Mentioned in relation to his 500th home run, which brightened Manny's day.

Mike Cvetkovich (deceased): Aunt Dot's ex-husband, whom she divorced after eighteen years of marriage.

Mort Shulman (deceased): He was is a significant figure in Diana's life, a well-known businessman in Montreal who had complex ties with her family, revealing crucial information about her mother, Donna, and playing a pivotal role in her journey to uncover family secrets.

Mrs. Kenvyn (deceased): The first tenant of the Sylvia Hotel (historical mention).

Nancy Flamm (deceased): Michele's mother, who looked after Alex and David during a dinner outing in Las Vegas.

Orland McConnell (deceased): Diana's uncle by marriage, who lived in Burnaby, BC. Known for his friendly demeanor and career in horse grooming and training, Orland was a significant presence in Diana's family life.

Paul and Mary: Diana's biological maternal great-grandparents, mentioned by Grandmother.

Petrillo brothers (deceased): The brothers were friends with the Filippone family in Vancouver. My Aunt Jan told me that one of the brothers might be my biological father, who lives in North Vancouver.

Phyllis Corbie (deceased): Brent's mother who passed away the week Diana moved to Denver.

Pierre Trudeau (deceased) Former Prime Minister of Canada, mentioned in a photo.

Priest: The priest in Montreal, whom Diana spoke with at the Notre Dame Basilica, shared insights about the struggles of pregnant single women in the 1950s.

Queen Elizabeth and the Duke of Edinburgh (both deceased): Seen in one of the films.

Rabbi Hershom: Chief Rabbi who managed Congregation Shiloh, across the street from where Donna lived in Montreal.

Ramon Castro (deceased): Another member of Castro's family mentioned in the photos.

Raul Castro: Cuban leader, confirmed to be in the photos.

Regina (deceased): A resident at Legacy Senior Center who comments on her familiarity with Diana's mother.

Rev. Bob Burrows: A minister at the First United Church who provides Diana with information and a tour of the church.

Rich Uhrlaub: Adoptee and activist from ASRC who helped open birth records in Colorado. He advocates for adoptee rights and has provided Diana with valuable knowledge and support.

Richard Kreedman: Diana's best friend's husband, who suggests they meet in Las Vegas for a few days to help Diana cope with her husband's sudden death.

Rick McCartie: A friend of Diana who helps with her research and accompanies her throughout Vancouver.

Roberta Hochberg: Daughter of Abraham and Anna Hochberg, and Diana's adopted cousin.

Rod Hourston (deceased): James's father, a former biologist and WWII bomber pilot who resides at Legacy Senior Center.

Rosemary: Jesse's biological sister, who was unaware of his existence until Diana reached out.

Ruby Wilkinson-Pauldino-Teague-Keller (deceased): Ruby is Diana's grandmother who has been married multiple times, playing a significant role in Diana's paternal lineage.

Sam Monroe: Sam Monroe is the husband of Stacey Monroe, a close friend of the author Diana, and he works as a merchant seaman whose life involves frequent and extended absences due to his job on a submarine.

Sean Holman: An investigative journalist and documentary filmmaker suggested by John for Diana to contact.

Stacey Monroe: She is a close friend of the author Diana Kayla Hochberg, who has been involved in Diana's life and stories since the spring of 1988.

Stacey Sanders: Founder of Elevating Connections, befriends Diana. Elevating Connections focuses on reuniting siblings separated by the foster care system, and Stacey's dedication resonates with Diana, forming a strong friendship.

Stephanie Bellfy: A woman from Indiana who manages her deceased brother Dustin Overmyer's account and becomes a contact for Diana.

Steve Lincoln: Diana's closest friend, confidant, providing her with guidance and support both professionally and personally.

Steve/Stephen Whiteman (deceased): Diana's husband, who died in a car accident in Palm Springs, Ca. Father of Claire Marie Whiteman.

Stu Miller (deceased): The pitcher against whom Mickey Mantle hit his 500th home run.

Sylvia Klein (deceased): The wife of Joe Klein, mentioned in the love letter he wrote to Diana's father.

Sylvia Ronahan: Gabriel wife in Burnaby, BC.

Ted Harrison: Cheryl's husband.

Thelma: James Van Velson's wife.

Tom Needes: A neighbor mentioned who knew Diana's Grandmother Annie on Parker Street.

Uncle Ronald, Ron Kolosky (deceased): Uncle Ronald, also known as Ron Kolosky, was my biological uncle on the maternal side. He was a former lumberjack who lived on Vancouver Island.

Uncle Tom/Thomas Fredrick Koloski (also known as Freddie) (deceased): Diana's biological maternal uncle, Tom who was also known as Freddie, was fluent in multiple languages and traveled extensively. He cared for Diana's grandmother until her passing and continued living in the family home until his death in 2010.

Vince Chessa (deceased): A man with connections to the Penthouse Nightclub and the Rizzuto family, mentioned in a conversation with John.

Walter Rae: A clairvoyant and former pilot who shares his stories and helps Diana with her search.

## APPENDIX B
Persons in *Connected* whose names have been changed

Adelaide: Special Collections Librarian at the Vancouver Public Library who helps Diana locate the magazine article.

Adele Wiseman (deceased): Donna rented a room for three years from Adele while attending college in Montreal.

Anastasia: A woman at the United Ukrainian Hall of Canada who welcomes Diana and helps her learn about the community.

Andrew Chen: An advisor at Forest Lawn Funeral Home who helps Diana with her inquiries will

Bonnie Route: Fran's granddaughter, living in the house to help Fran out.

Bookstore Owner: The woman who owns the longest-standing family-owned bookstore in Sarasota.

Brando: Owner of Cafe Calabria who recognizes Donna's photo.

Bruno: An older gentleman who comes into Diana's work establishment and confides in her about his mob ties and requests a custom signet ring.

Charmaine: A contact who helps Diana connect with Liam and provides information about Joe Gentile.

Chef Massimo: He is a renowned Italian chef and restaurateur based in Vancouver, British Columbia. He may recognize Diana's mother from a photo.

Cherie: An expert in connecting with people through messages on Ancestry.

Collin: The Hourston family's attorney, who advises Diana on her legal rights and family matters.

Dakota: Diana's friend from North Carolina.

Dean: A single parent and friend of Diana who she met at David's Tae Kwon Do class; he offers advice and support during her journey.

Detective Alexander: A police detective who follows and helps Diana during her trip to Victoria.

Detective Constable Daniel Murphy: A Vancouver police officer investigating Diana's mother's case.

Dr. Claude Hardwick (deceased): The doctor who signed Donna's Registration of Death and provided information about her last days.

Emma Preston: Mort's daughter.

Esther (deceased): Diana's adopted mom's cousin.

Gabrielle: The woman who purchased Diana's grandmother's house in Vancouver, BC, Canada.

Genevieve Route: Bio Paternal cousin

Hampton Preston: Mort's nephew who contacts Diana about their potential family connection.

Hans: Funeral director at Forest Lawn Funeral Home and Memorial Park in Burnaby.

Henry Abbott: An immigration lawyer based in Montreal, known for represented Mort Shulman.

Jacob: The adopted son of Gabrielle.

Jacqueline: A new friend and fellow teacher who moved from Pennsylvania to South Carolina, helping Diana with computer writing programs.

Jay Preston (deceased): Mort's father and a business colleague of Manny Hochberg.

Jon Russo (deceased): Diana's father's close friend and foreperson, who reveals information about Diana's adoption and the day her father was driven somewhere, contributing to the mystery surrounding her origins.

Josh: was adopted by Fran and her late husband John Route.

Joy: Diana's childhood friend from New York City.

Kenji: The manager of "The Art of Hair," a notable establishment.

Leonardo Parisi: A historian in Vancouver's Italian community, whom Liam and Diana contact for help with their research.

Liam Cross: An entrepreneur and researcher of Vancouver's Mafia history, who initially helps Diana.

Luca: Michael Pauldino's son who provides Diana and Eric with information about their family history through email.

Luis: Victor's brother-in-law, who provides insights into a film with historical figures.

Mario A.: Diana's newly discovered first cousin from her paternal side, who contacted her through Ancestry.

Mary (Marigold) Hardwick (deceased): Dr. Hardwick's wife, who assists in the conversation and provides additional insights.

Maurice Kimble: Health Record manager for Vancouver General Hospital.

Mysterious Caller: The killer voice on the phone was an anonymous, threatening figure whose calls instilled fear and added suspense to the story.

Nathan Costello (deceased): Diana's father's lawyer for over forty years, involved in handling her father's legal matters and estate.

Nina Carnes: Michael Pauldino's wife.

Paul: The bartender at Gaetano.

Pete: Friend of Ed Cosgrove in Port Moody.

Police Officer at Station: Greets Diana and informs her about scheduling an appointment with Detective Constable Daniel Murphy.

Police Officers: Unnamed officers who give Diana a suggestion in Ybor City.

Randy: Diana's caseworker at Vital Records in Albany, who assists her with obtaining her birth certificates and navigating the complexities of her adoption records.

Receptionist: The person who gives Diana Billy Cox's email address at the *Sarasota Herald-Tribune*.

Rex: Diana's friend with connections in Washington, D.C.

Rosalind Costello (deceased): The wife of Nathan Costello, who informs Diana about her husband's death and offers to help find information about her adoption.

Scarlett Wiseman: Adele's adopted daughter.

Señor Diaz: Desi Diaz, referred to more formally at first. Desi Diaz: The owner of a cigar shop in Ybor City.

Sofia: Michael Pauldino's daughter who contacts Diana after Eric reaches out to her.

Stella: A woman from Vancouver who provides Diana with information about black-market adoptions and legal advice.

Stuart: My adopted cousin's husband from Maryland.

Susan and Eve: Diana's adoptive cousins.

Taylor: Friend and co-moderator of Diana's photography group, helping her research hypoallergenic cats.

The unknown man: The third man who brought Diana's mother to Vancouver General Hospital in May 1967.

The unknown man: The third man who was with Joe Gentile and James Sanseverino on the night Donna was taken to the hospital.

Unidentified man in the bathing trunks: Mentioned in the Cuba film shared by Diana.

Unnamed Man Behind the Curtain: An older man who recognizes people in the photos.

Vancouver Library Librarian: Librarian Assists the Diana in the Special Collections Department, guiding her to microfiche readers for family history research.

Victor and Catalina: Diana's friends who host her during the holidays and support her writing journey.

Vivian Abbott: Henry Abbott's wife and has been acting as his secretary since 1981.

Wanda: The hotel salon receptionist who interacts with Diana's father and is involved in a story about Diana and Michele's misadventures in Las Vegas.

Wayne: The son of Joe Gentile, the owner of a coffee shop that Diana visits.

Zoe: A staff member at a photography shop who helps Diana with the film conversion.

# REFERENCES

Reputable DNA sites I used:

- Ancestry.com.
- 23and Me.com
- Family Tree.com
- GEDmatch.com

Information Search Resources and Internet Resources used in my research

- Ancestry.com Resource records
- Canada.archives.com (search records free)
- GEDmatch offers a free DNA site built for genetic genealogy research
- British Columbia Genealogical Society - Member
- National Genealogical Society - Member
- Archives in New Westminster - New Westminster, Canada
- Archives in Vancouver - Vancouver, B.C. Canada
- Clearwater Main Library, Clearwater, Florida
- Denver Public Library, Denver, Colorado
- New Westminster Library, Vancouver, Canada
- Safety Harbor Library, Safety Harbor, Florida
- Selby Public Library, Sarasota, Florida
- Special Collections | Vancouver Public Library, Vancouver, BC Canada
- The Western History & Genealogy Department, Denver, Colorado
- Vancouver Public Library, Central Library - Downtown Vancouver, BC Canada

- Manhattan General Hospital - Manhattan, New York
- Royal Columbian Hospital - New Westminster, BC Canada
- Vancouver General Hospital - Vancouver, BC Canada

Books Mentioned in *Connected*
- *Hidden History of St. Petersburg* by Will Michaels
- *Hope Lives Here* by Bob Burrows
- *Liquor, Lust, and the Law* by Aaron Chapman
- *Mob Rule: Inside the Canadian Mafia* by James Dubro
- *Smaldone: The Untold Story of an American Crime Family* by Dick Kreck
- *The Traffic in Babies: Cross-Border Adoption and Baby-Selling between the United States and Canada, 1930-1972* by Karen Balcom

Songs Mentioned in *Connected*
- "Girls Just Want to Have Fun" by Cyndi Lauper
- "I Will Survive" by Gloria Gaynor
- "My Way" by Frank Sinatra

Films Mentioned in *Connected*
- *Father Unknown 2014* - Documentary/Drama directed by David Quint
- *It's a Wonderful Life*
- *Miracle on 34th Street*
- *The Godfather* (Film)
- *The Goodfellas* (Film)
- *True Lies* (1994 Film)
- *The Sopranos*

Social Media Groups, Additional Resources, and Podcasts
- Adoption Search Research Connection ASRC https://www.asrconline.org/
- Anderson, D. (n.d.). Missing Pieces - NPE Life Podcast. https://missingpieces.buzzsprout.com/

- Celia Center Inc. https://celiacenter.org/
- DNA Identity Surprise and This NPE Life https://www.facebook.com/groups/thisnpelife
- DNAngels. https://www.dnangels.org
- Family Twist Podcast. Hosted by Corey Cottrell and Kendall Hopkins. https://www.familytwistpodcast.com
- Fireside Adoptees. (n.d.) Fireside Adoptees Facebook Group. https://www.facebook.com/groups/1411791922534076
- Forum for Late-Discovery Adoptees https://www.facebook.com/groups/latediscoveryadoptees/
- InterCountry Adoptee Voices (ICAV) https://www.facebook.com/groups/Intercountryadopteevoices
- MPE Life: DNA Surprise, NPE, Adoptees, & Donor Conceived (DCP): https://www.facebook.com/groups/mpelife/
- NAAP Official Website https://naapunited.org/adoption-happy-hour
- National Association of Adoptees and Parents https://naapunited.org/
- Nursing for npes www.nursingfornpes.com
- Reckoning with The Primal Wound. Directed by Rebecca Autumn Sansom. https://www.reckoningwiththeprimalwound.com/
- Right To Know: https://righttoknow.us/
- Saving Our Sisters associated with Renee Gelin https://savingoursistersadoption.org
- Society for Adoption Truth https://www.societyforadoptiontruth.org/
- The Gathering Place https://www.facebook.com/groups/233642325392416
- The Thriving Adoptees Simon Benn Podcast https://www.facebook.com/thrivingadoptees
- Untangling Our Roots https://untanglingourroots.org/

# ACKNOWLEDGMENTS

I would like to extend my heartfelt gratitude to Linda Ketron, editor and publisher at CLASS LLC, for believing in me and the vision behind *Connected: Finding My Truth*. From the very beginning, Linda, you saw the heart of this project and understood its deep personal significance. Your tireless dedication, insightful guidance, and unwavering support ensured that this book would reach readers in the most meaningful way. Working with you has been an honor, and I am profoundly grateful for the trust you placed in me and this journey.

I would also like to recognize the incredible CLASS team, whose expertise and hard work brought this project to life. Sherri Estridge, your talent as a graphic designer and your meticulous attention to detail as an editorial assistant ensured that every aspect of the book's presentation was polished and professional. Anne Swift Malarich, your skillful photography editing added visual depth and clarity, elevating the book's overall impact.

To Linda, Sherri, and Anne—your collective dedication, creativity, and professionalism have made this book a reality. I am deeply thankful for each of you and the role you played in bringing *Connected: Finding My Truth* to life.

My heartfelt thanks to Dr. Jason C. Rosenberg for his thoughtful foreword, which beautifully captures the themes of inquiry and resilience at the heart of this book. His insights and reflections have enriched this narrative, offering readers a meaningful entry point into my story. Dr. Rosenberg's support and intellectual generosity have been invaluable, and I am deeply grateful.

David, you are not just my son; you are my confidant, my mentor, and my greatest source of strength. Your boundless love and unwavering belief in me have been my anchor through every challenge. From our late-night conversations to the quiet moments of comfort when I needed them most, you have always reminded me of the power of love and resilience.

Walking this journey with you and witnessing the incredible person you are is a privilege beyond measure. Thank you for embodying everything good in this world and for standing by me through it all. I am endlessly proud to call you, my son.

With all my love and admiration,

Mom

I am deeply grateful for my daughter-in-law, Erica, whose intelligence, drive, and kindness inspire everyone she meets. You are not only a steadfast rock for my son but also a true partner in every sense, bringing balance, joy, and meaning to his life. With the arrival of precious Harper, you have embraced motherhood with such grace and love, enriching our family in ways words cannot express. Thank you for being the light in his world, the princess of his castle, and for welcoming us all into this beautiful new chapter with open arms.

I am so grateful to my brother Jesse for protecting me in my early years. encouraging me to finish writing my book, and sharing bits of his own story within it. I hope he find the true peace and happiness within himself.

I would like to acknowledge my stepdaughter, Claire Whiteman, who lives in Germany. Though we now connect mainly through live chats and social media, the treasured memories of your childhood remain etched in my heart. Seeing the incredible person, you've grown into fills me with pride and joy, even from afar.

Thank you, Steve Lincoln, for always having faith in me and being my best friend. Our paths crossed in 1987, when you began your career as an air traffic controller for the FAA in Sarasota, Florida. Through every difficulty and achievement, you've been by my side, offering unconditional love, encouragement that gave me the courage to undertake this journey. You are more than a friend; you are family and my biggest supporter.

Throughout the writing of my book, my friend Mina Nix provided invaluable support. She listened attentively, I am deeply grateful for her guidance and friendship.

Thanks to Cheryl Sweeney for beta-reading my manuscript. I appreciate your constructive feedback and suggestions, which significantly improved my work. I'm also grateful to my dear friends and family who took the time to read a few of my chapters and offered valuable insights when I felt stuck. In particular, I express my heartfelt appreciation to Erica Hochberg, Brent Corbie, Katy Wolf, Jennifer Cabraja, Jimmy Steenland, Helene Albright, Donna Nordone, Barbara Mendelson, Monica Bland, and Denise Marie Arvelo, whose feedback was invaluable to me.

I want to express my gratitude to a group of amazing people who have been instrumental in helping me share my mother's story. Ethan Baron, a reporter at the *Mercury News*, captured my attention with an outstanding article about my mom in August 2009. I'm also grateful to Daphne Bramham, a retired columnist from *The Vancouver Sun*, for her unwavering support. Billy Cox, a former reporter at the *Sarasota Herald-Tribune*, continuously motivated me with his kind words of encouragement. My thanks extend to Jana G. Pruden, a feature writer at *The Globe and Mail*, who generously shared one of my mother's stories. Sean Holman, a well-known online investigative journalist and documentary filmmaker in British Columbia, was incredibly helpful in making connections. Special gratitude goes to Gordon Clark, a former reporter at the *Vancouver Sun and Province*, for his invaluable assistance. Cristina Puig, an award-winning news anchor based in Tampa, Florida, has expressed a keen interest in exploring my mother's story in Cuba, and I'm excited about the opportunity to talk to her. Noel Brennan from Denver News 9, thank you for doing the segment on "Storytellers: Adoptees Share Secrets, Search for Family." I'm also thankful to Elaine Cobiella-Strong, a retired writer and editor from *The Gazette Colorado Springs Newspaper*, for her words of encouragement after our extensive discussions over coffee. Finally, I wish to thank Carolyn Soltau, a research librarian at the *Vancouver Sun and Province* Newsroom, for her assistance in obtaining photos of my mother. I look forward to our interview and cannot thank everyone enough for their support.

I am deeply thankful to Ancestry, 23andMe, and GEDmatch for their invaluable contributions to my DNA journey. Their services have provided me with the most comprehensive and enriching experience in connecting with my ancestors. I am also grateful to Janice Johnston for sharing her expertise in building family trees and teaching me how to assist others in discovering their ancestors. My gratitude extends to my cousin, James Van Velson, whose excellent work has brought our family history to life with his expertise and attention to detail. Additionally, during my return from the Summit 'Untangling Our Roots' held in Louisville in the spring of 2023, I connected with my cousin, Bettye Horton Bunch, who shared her genealogy expertise and shed light on our family history. I must also extend my deep appreciation to Professor Karen Balcom, who has done extensive work on the sale of Black-Market Babies in Montreal. Her research and insights have added a crucial dimension to understanding our collective past.

Thank you to all the new family members who have enriched my life. A special thanks to Gabriel Mark Hasselbach, the unparalleled horn maestro, and his lovely wife, Sylvia Ronahan. You welcomed me into your home in Canada and encouraged me to think outside the box, exploring horizons beyond what I knew from my mother's story. To Cheryl Harrison, my first cousin on the paternal side, thank you for agreeing to do your DNA test and for sharing all the fascinating stories about our families. And yes, I remember that your middle name is Jeanette. Thank you, Eric Teague, for reaching out to me and convincing me of our connection on Ancestry through my paternal grandmother. I am also deeply grateful for Uncle Kenny Teague, whom I met after his 83rd birthday. Thank you for so warmly welcoming me into your family; I feel incredibly fortunate to have you in my life. Thank you, David Quint, for accompanying me to meet my new cousins in Denver. It was a heartwarming experience.

To the Pawleys Island community, thank you for making me feel like family. A special thanks to the Waccamaw Neck Arts Alliance, the artists, neighbors, and friends who have enriched my life here—especially my first friend, Diane Smith.

"Gatsby," thank you for helping me complete my manuscript. Your presence and encouraging meows kept me motivated.

I am deeply grateful to my adoptive family for embracing me as one of their own, without any discrimination. In fact, many of my cousins were not even aware of my adoption. Additionally, I wish to express my appreciation to my biological family and cousins who have recently connected with me; together, we are now working on building our friendships.

I am also thankful for my childhood friends, for the memories and connections we forged in our youth, and for the significance these relationships still hold as we grow older. My heartfelt thanks go to Michele Kreedman, Ilene Neues, Elena Paperny, Lee Flaum, Lynne Flaum, Julie MacNeil, Claude Cathcart, Cindy Edwards, Sue Paszkowski, Linda Hunt, Frank De Benedittis, Zippora Levy, Allen Levy, Marla Dillon, Laura Levine, Bonnie Mannheimer, Marilyn Fishman, Harriet Weissman, David Levy, Francey Levy, Linda Gavette, and Laurie Morrison for being such an integral part of my life and for the special moments we have shared.

I am grateful for the support extended by the adoption community. Your kindness, compassion, and presence have been a tremendous source of comfort for me. I cannot thank you enough for your invaluable positive influence. I want to express my gratitude to Alesia Weiss, Alicia Williams, Ann Marie, Ann Mikeska, Barbara Robertson, Beth Steury, Beth Syverson, Brad Ewell, Cassandra Adams, Corey Stulce, Damon Davis, David B. Bohl, David Quint, Don Anderson, Donna Lipka, Dr. Abby Hasberry, Dr. Joyce Maguire Pavao, Emma Stevens, Fred Firestine, Fred Nicora, Greg Gentry, Jack Rocco, Jacoba Ballard, Jean Kelly Widner, Jennifer Fahlsing, Juli Petrie Gallup, Kara Rubinstein Deyerin, Kendall Stulce, Lauren Balaban, Leslie MacKinnon, Marci Purcell, Marcie Keithley, Maria Leonard Olsen, Mary Ann Scott, Melissa Brunetti, Michele Kriegman, Michelle Tullier, Monica Bland,

Monica Hall, Moses Farrow, Nancy McCaughey, Paul Jack Fronczak, Peter Capomolla Moore, Peter J. Boni, Rebecca Autumn Sansom, Renee Gelin, Richard Uhrlaub, Shelley Dunlap Johnson, Shelley Hamilton, Shirley Muñoz Newson, Simon Benn, Susan Ross, Tiana Neshama, Vin Adoptee Jarrod, and many others who have been there for me. To anyone I may have unintentionally omitted, please know that your support and contributions have not gone unnoticed, and I am deeply grateful for your kindness and encouragement.

My family, friends, and social media followers have been an incredible source of support and inspiration for me for over seven years. I am incredibly grateful for their encouragement and influence, which have been instrumental in shaping who I am today. I want to express my sincere thanks to each one of them for being there for me.

My deepest thank you to everyone who struggles with questions about their families and identities. Your persistence and courage so inspire me, and I pray you all find the answers you need to live your life and be happy.

I want to thank God, life, and the universe for everyone and everything I experienced during my journey.

## IN MEMORIAM

In memory of those who have contributed to my life and this book, thank you. Though you are gone from sight, you will forever remain in my heart.

Abraham Hochberg: 1906-1980
Anita Small: 1936-2017
Ann Gister: 1915-2012
Anna Hochberg: 1909-1989
Anne May: 1938-2019
Annie Bilyk-Koloski: 1910-2000
Ava Lee Millman Fisher: 1946-2022

Barry Peacock: 1956-2018
Bonnie Garramone: 1928-May 29,2023
Dennis Blewitt: 1943-October 29, 2023
Dermod Travis: 1960-2020
Doris Langerak: Sept 9, 1932-2019
Dot Koloski-Cvetkovich: 1934-2019
Dustin Overmyer: 1983-2017
Ed Cosgrove: 1926-1992
Ethel Hochberg: 1915-1966
Frances Lillian Route: 1939-2022
Frank aka Fred Koloski: 1906-1973
Freddie aka Tom Koloski: 1931-2010
James Roger Hourston: 1956-2023
Jan Kolosky-McConnell: 1931-2017
Jean Balanik-Kolosky: 1943-2016
Joe Klein: 1910-1995
Kathy Ann White-Fuller: 1944-2015
Kris Secrest: 1958-2019
Lily Grouix: 1934-2020
Lorraine Sansing: 1925-2019
Manny Diamond: 1917-1995
Manny Hochberg: 1910-1979
Marty (Marlene) Holmes: 1939-2008
Millie Cohen: 1928-2019
Mort Shulman: 1925-2012
Nancy Flamm: 1919-2009
Orland McConnell: 1925-2014
Perry Staiano: 1958-2021
Phyllis Corbie: 1930-2017
Rebecca Hochberg: 1902-1983
Ronald Kolosky: 1932-2020
Ronald Thaler: 1928-2019
Sylvia Klein: 1910-1982
William Roderick (Rod) Hourston: 1922-2018

## ABOUT THE AUTHOR

DIANA KAYLA HOCHBERG is an accomplished photographer with more than twenty-five years of experience in retail management and twenty years as an educator. Her life is a testament to the power of self-discovery and perseverance.

Diana was born in Montreal, Canada, and raised in New York. She holds a Bachelor's Degree in Education and an Associate of Arts degree in Art History. Since 2017, she has been a member of the British Columbia Genealogical Society and the National Genealogical Society. Diana is passionate about genealogy and helping adoptees and non-adoptees discover their family histories.

She is the proud mother of son David, daughter-in-law Erica, and granddaughter Harper, as well as her stepdaughter Claire. Diana resides in Pawleys Island, South Carolina, with her brother Jesse and her Siberian cat Gatsby.

*Connected: Finding My Truth* is Diana's debut book.

### Giving Back

A portion of all proceeds or royalties from the sales of this book will be donated to the following organizations: *National Association of Adoptees and Parents, Inc., Society for Adoption Truth*, and *Saving Our Sisters*.